Gender Equality and Social Justice: Striving for a Balanced World

Ayesha Siddiqui

Copyright © [2023] by Ayesha Siddiqui

All rights reserved. No part of this publication may be reproduced, distributed, or transmitted in any form or by any means, including photocopying, recording, or other electronic or mechanical methods, without the prior written permission of the publisher, except in the case of brief quotations embodied in critical reviews and certain other noncommercial uses permitted by copyright law

Author: Ayesha Siddiqui

Title: Gender Equality and Social Justice: Striving for a Balanced World

Cover design by Miss Kaveri

Interior layout and design by Mr. Samar

Disclaimer:
The views and opinions expressed in this book are those of the author and do not necessarily reflect the official policy or position of any other agency, organization, employer, or company. Assumptions made in the analysis are not reflective of the position of any entity other than the author.

ISBN: 978-93-5868-462-9

Table Of Content

Chapter 1:
Introduction to Gender Equality and Social Justice...........................05
- Definition and importance of gender equality and social justice
- Historical overview of gender inequality and social injustice
- The impact of gender inequality on societies and economies
- Key concepts and terms: patriarchy, intersectionality, gender stereotypes

Chapter 2:
Understanding the Roots of Gender Inequality.................................23
- Exploration of cultural and societal norms shaping gender roles
- Analysis of the impact of media and popular culture on gender perceptions
- Examination of religious and traditional beliefs influencing gender discrimination
- Case studies showcasing gender disparities in various cultures and regions

Chapter 3:
Intersectionality: Overlapping Identities and Inequalities..................40
- Definition and significance of intersectionality in the context of gender equality
- Exploration of how race, class, sexuality, and other factors intersect with gender
- Real-life examples illustrating the complexities of intersectional discrimination
- Strategies for addressing intersectional inequalities and promoting inclusivity

Chapter 4:
Women's Empowerment and Economic Justice..............................59
- ➢ Overview of economic disparities between genders
- ➢ Analysis of workplace discrimination and the gender pay gap
- ➢ Examination of women's entrepreneurship and financial inclusion
- ➢ Initiatives and policies promoting women's economic empowerment

Chapter 5:
Social Justice Movements and Policy Interventions............................78
- ➢ Historical overview of feminist movements and their impact on society
- ➢ Analysis of successful gender equality policies implemented globally
- ➢ Exploration of grassroots movements and their role in promoting social justice
- ➢ Case studies of countries or regions making significant progress in gender equality

Chapter 6:
Building a Balanced Future: Challenges and Opportunities................98
- ➢ Current challenges in achieving gender equality and social justice
- ➢ Analysis of the role of education and awareness in fostering change
- ➢ Exploration of the potential of technology in advancing gender equality
- ➢ Strategies and recommendations for individuals, communities, and governments to promote a balanced world

Conclusion...119

Chapter 1: Introduction to Gender Equality and Social Justice

➢ Definition and importance of gender equality and social justice

A fair and equitable society is predicated on the pillars of gender parity and social justice. What we mean by "gender equality" is that people of both sexes should have the same access to resources and opportunities. It means that the differences between women and men are acknowledged and respected, as well as their interests, needs, and priorities. On the other side, social justice refers to the practice of ensuring that everyone in a society has access to the same opportunities and resources. This essay explores the meanings and relevance of gender equality and social justice, demonstrating how they are intertwined and essential to the development of a progressive and peaceful society.

Equality between the sexes: A Definition
Gender equality is not limited to the rights of women; rather, it is a universal human right that protects all people from discrimination on the basis of their gender. It entails ensuring that men and women have equal access to educational and occupational opportunities as well as to positions of power in society. Gender equality works to dismantle the societal conventions and prejudices that are based on gender. The movement supports women's and girls' rights and demands that men and women be treated equally.

The Meaning of "Social Justice"

Fair and equitable allocation of society's resources, opportunities, and privileges are all aspects of social justice. It necessitates acknowledging and resolving the enduring economic inequities, racial, ethnic, gender, sexual orientation, and socioeconomic discrimination that exist in a variety of ways. For social justice advocates, the end goal is a society in which people of all identities and socioeconomic backgrounds enjoy the same opportunities and protections under the law. Its goals include the complete elimination of poverty, the expansion of opportunities for all people, and the protection of everyone's inherent worth.

The Link Between Social Justice and Gender Equality

Gender equality and social justice are inextricably interwoven. In order to attain social justice, it is necessary to combat pervasive forms of discrimination and inequality based on gender. Women and members of other marginalized groups continue to face barriers to advancement in areas including education, work, and healthcare because of discrimination. Equal rights and opportunities for all people, regardless of their gender identity, are essential components of social justice, which can be furthered by efforts to achieve gender equality.

Furthermore, attempts to promote gender equality are frequently included in social justice efforts that target underprivileged areas. For instance, empowering women in low-income communities helps reduce poverty and advance society as a whole, all while addressing the issue of gender inequality. The development of holistic methods to achieve an inclusive and just society requires an understanding of the interdependence of gender equality and social justice.

The Value of Social Justice and Gender Equality
Promoting Economic success: Gender equality in the workplace leads to a diversified and talented workforce, fostering innovation and economic success. Women's equal access to the workforce increases productivity and positively impacts the economy.

Gender equality in education improves the educational opportunities for both girls and boys. In order to end the cycle of poverty and foster social progress, it is essential that women have an education.
Promoting Health and Well-Being: Gender Equity in Healthcare Guarantees Access to Quality Care for All People. Improved health outcomes are the result of its focus on topics including maternal mortality, reproductive health, and violence against women.

Contributing to Stronger Communities Gender equality encourages women to take part in political and economic decision-making at all levels of society. Women's participation in political leadership and policymaking improves the quality of decisions made on behalf of the entire population.

Violence and discrimination against women are also reduced thanks to efforts to promote gender equality. Society can become more accepting and courteous of people of different gender identities and expressions if we work to dismantle damaging preconceptions and standards.

Resolving Conflicts and Constructing Peaceful Societies: The Role of Gender Equality. Peace agreements that can withstand the test of time are more likely to be reached when women have a voice in the negotiation process.

Promoting Social Unity: Social justice, especially gender equality, helps bring people together by leveling the playing field and making sure that everyone has a fair shot at success. As a result, people from all walks of life are better able to live in peace and harmony with one another.

The United Nations' Sustainable Development Goals (SDGs) include a focus on gender parity and social justice. The entire goal of sustainable development cannot be realized without progress toward gender equality (Goal 5) and the promotion of peace, justice, and strong institutions (Goal 16).

Conclusion
Social justice and gender parity are not mere ideals; they form the bedrock of a just and progressive society. By eliminating bias and providing equal chances for people of all genders, we can tap into the entire creative potential of our society. Gender equality and social justice must be actively promoted and advocated for by governments, organizations, and individuals. Doing so can help bring about a world in which all people, regardless of their background or identity, are treated with equality and respect, have equal access to resources, and

experience social justice in their daily lives. A better future for everyone can be achieved by accepting and advocating for these values.

➤ Historical overview of gender inequality and social injustice

Introduction

Gender bias and social unfairness are pervasive problems that have been around for a long time and may be found in every culture and civilization. This essay offers a thorough examination of the historical development, symptoms, and causes of gender inequality and social injustice. To comprehend the intricate relationship between social, cultural, economic, and political elements that has sustained these disparities over time, an examination of the historical backdrop is essential. Learning about the difficulties and successes of earlier cultures is a key benefit of historical research.

Gender Roles in Ancient Societies

In ancient civilizations, gender roles were generally tightly delineated, with women consigned to domestic domains while men occupied positions of power and control. Women, for instance, were not allowed to hold public office or participate in political life in ancient Greece. Similarly, Confucianism in ancient China upheld patriarchal values by emphasizing men's superiority over women. These early societies set the stage for generations of inequality by laying the groundwork for rigid gender roles.

The Middle Ages and Feudalism

Feudal rules and practices in Europe during that time period contributed to and reinforced the existing gender gap. Women were considered the property of their husbands and had very limited legal rights. The Church was essential in defining cultural norms, and it frequently propagated the view that women were inferior to males while also elevating their status as primary caregivers and mothers. Similar patterns of gender inequality remained in many other parts of the world, with societal conventions and religious beliefs severely limiting women's rights.

Gender disparity and social injustice were both exacerbated during the colonial era. Many indigenous gender roles and forms of government were weakened as European colonial powers pushed their own values on the region. Women in colonized areas were often subjected to prejudice, abuse, and exploitation. The legacy of colonialism continues to influence social dynamics and gender relations in numerous regions of the world, illustrating the continuing impact of historical injustices.

The Fight for Women's Equality in the 19th and 20th Centuries
Many social and political movements in the 19th and 20th centuries fought for equal rights for women. An important turning point in the fight for women's rights, the suffragette movement was especially active in Europe and North America. Many countries of the world only recently began to recognize women's rights after activists fought against discriminatory legislation and pushed for legislative reforms.

Changes in Women's Roles Caused by Industrialization
Traditional gender norms were challenged by the industrial revolution, which also opened doors for women to enter the workforce. Some women were able to enter the workforce

because of the industrial revolution, but they endured dangerous circumstances and few protections. The rise of feminist movements in the late 19th and early 20th centuries pushed for women's economic, political, and social rights, establishing the framework for future achievements in gender equality.

Social Justice and Feminist Movements after WWII

Feminist movements sprang up all across the world in the wake of World War II. Women's rights campaigners called for an end to violence against women and the right to choose one's own reproductive health care. The United Nations' international conventions and declarations did a lot to advance the cause of gender parity. The development of groups like UN Women demonstrated the world's dedication to improving the status of women and achieving greater social fairness.

The 21st Century: Perils and Achievements

There has been a lot of improvement in the last few decades, but issues of gender inequality and social injustice still exist. Women still have less access to education and training, earn less than men, and are underrepresented in positions of power. Domestic violence, as well as sexual assault and human trafficking, are still serious problems in many countries. The interconnectedness of gender inequality with other forms of discrimination is further highlighted by the fact that marginalized communities, especially LGBTQ+ individuals, endure discrimination and societal injustices.

In the 21st century, there have been major efforts to overcome these difficulties. Gender equality has advanced in many spheres thanks to public education, advocacy, and legislative changes. Progress has been made in many nations thanks to programs that encourage the education of girls, economic independence for women, and political representation of women. Important discussions regarding consent, power dynamics, and responsibility have been sparked by the MeToo movement and other grassroots efforts to bring attention to sexual harassment and assault.

Conclusion
The long and difficult road toward establishing equality for all persons, regardless of gender or identity, is shown by the historical review of gender inequality and social injustice. Although some advancement has been made, there is still a long way to go. If we want to build a society where everyone is treated fairly, we must confront long-held beliefs, combat discrimination, and advocate for policies that include everyone.

A fresh dedication to gender equality and social justice can propel nations ahead if they take stock of their historical context and draw lessons from past battles and accomplishments. The continued importance of education, knowledge, and activism in eradicating systemic disparities and creating a world in which everyone is accorded the same respect, decency, and justice is undeniable. The injustices of the past can be corrected and a more just and inclusive future can be established if people work together and remain committed to human rights.

➤ The impact of gender inequality on societies and economies

Gender inequality, a profoundly ingrained issue in cultures worldwide, has far-reaching implications that extend beyond individual lives. Not only do women feel the effects of this, but so do their families, their communities, and even their country's economy as a whole. This essay investigates the many facets of gender inequality and the far-reaching effects it has on societies, economics, and human progress. Recognizing the need of eliminating gender inequality and constructing more equitable and affluent communities requires an appreciation of these effects.

1. Impoverishment and Financial Insecurity

Economic disempowerment, especially for women, is a direct result of gender inequity. Women's economic engagement is hampered by a lack of access to education and employment possibilities as well as by discriminatory behaviors. Women are disproportionately represented in the low-wage, informal economy, where they are vulnerable to exploitation and insecurity. Therefore, female-headed households are disproportionately represented among the poor. Individual potential is hampered, but economic progress is stunted as nations lose access to the skills and ideas of half their population as a result of economic disempowerment.

2. Skill Gaps and Achievement Gaps

In many regions of the world, gender inequality limits the opportunities available to female students. Disparities in access to higher education are more common for girls than for boys due to societal standards and economic factors. The potential of future female leaders, scientists, and inventors is wasted when girls are denied an education. Furthermore, inadequate educational possibilities reinforce skill gaps, hampering economic advancement by limiting the workforce's talents and innovation.

Maternal Mortality and Health Inequalities
Reproductive and maternal health are two aspects of women's health that are negatively impacted by gender inequality. Maternal mortality rates are greater in areas where sexism is widespread because women have less access to healthcare information and facilities. Furthermore, compared to men's health issues, those related to women's health generally receive little attention and money. As a result, societies incur higher healthcare expenses and see reduced output due to illnesses that could have been avoided.

4 Social Unrest and Violence Against Women
Gender inequality is a root cause of many forms of violence against women and girls. Violence against women not only inflicts physical and emotional harm but also creates fear and uncertainty. Gender-based violence creates social instability and slows growth in communities. Breaking the cycle of violence, building safer communities, and promoting social cohesion all require addressing gender inequity.

5. Inadequate Political Voice and Weak Influence

Political institutions that reflect gender inequality have a dearth of women in positions of power and influence. Policies may fail to meet the requirements of the people as a whole if women's views and viewpoints are not included in political processes. For inclusive governance, effective policymaking, and the advancement of social justice, gender parity in political representation is essential.

Implications for the Economy and Future Growth
Gender disparity has important economic ramifications, restricting the growth potential of economies. Recent studies have shown that narrowing the gender gap in the workforce and among business owners may boost global GDP by trillions. Economic equality allows countries to tap into a wide pool of talent and creativity, increasing productivity, innovation, and GDP development. Equal pay for equal work and encouragement of female business owners are two examples of gender-inclusive policies that have the potential to stimulate economic growth.

Creativity and problem-solving
Diversity in perspectives and experiences increases innovation and problem-solving capacities. Gender disparity reduces the number of perspectives that can be heard in many professions, STEM included. Society loses out on new ideas and perspectives when women are underrepresented in these spheres. Progress in society can be fueled by increasing the number of women working in STEM and other traditionally male-dominated sectors.

The Constraints of Society and Culture

Social and cultural conventions that prescribe traditional gender roles often contribute to the maintenance of gender inequity. Individuals' autonomy and agency are curtailed as a result, giving support to prejudice. It is crucial to dismantle gender inequality to challenge these conventions and promote gender equality in social and cultural domains. Societies that value and welcome difference produce more innovative thinkers, more tolerant citizens, and more respectful neighbors, all of which contribute to a more peaceful and prosperous society.

Conclusion

Gender inequality has far-reaching consequences for society and economies, touching on everything from individual well-being to national prosperity. When societies are aware of the many ways in which gender inequality manifests itself, they are more likely to make gender-inclusive laws and programs a top priority. In addition to fostering social justice, increasing women's access to education, employment, and political representation boosts economic growth and new ideas.

Governments, institutions, and individuals must all work together to reduce gender inequity. It is possible for societies to build a more just and prosperous future for all members of society if discriminatory practices are eradicated, old gender roles are questioned, and gender equality is promoted in all areas of society. Not only is it the moral thing to do for people of all genders, but it's also essential for creating societies that are strong, diverse, and prosperous. These initiatives allow civilizations to utilize their populations to their fullest capacity, paving the way for a better and more equal future.

➢ Key concepts and terms: patriarchy, intersectionality, gender stereotypes

Acquiring a firm understanding of foundational concepts and words is essential to mapping out the tangled terrain of gender dynamics and inequality. Fundamental ideas such as patriarchy, intersectionality, and gender stereotypes illuminate the complexity of gender-related issues. This essay discusses these notions in depth, deconstructing their meanings, origins, and consequences in contemporary culture.

1 Patriarchy: Dismantling the Status Quo
The term "patriarchy" is used to describe a societal structure in which men occupy positions of political and moral authority, social and economic privilege, and ownership of most material goods. It shapes cultural norms and structures to reflect the view that men are inherently superior than women and other gender identities.

The historical context of patriarchy may be found in ancient societies where men took up the positions of head of household, head of state, and head of business. Patriarchal regimes have persisted throughout history, affecting norms on the treatment of women and the rights of men.

Patriarchy has far-reaching effects on both individuals and communities. It hinders the advancement of underrepresented groups and is a major contributor to the persistence of gender-based violence. Furthermore, patriarchy reinforces oppressive gender norms by perpetuating negative assumptions and expectations that keep women in subordinate roles.

Intersectionality: Taking into Account Multiple Differences

An individual's race, ethnicity, financial background, sexual orientation, and gender identity all have a role in who they are, making up a complex and diverse whole. It acknowledges that people's identities often overlap and are intertwined in ways that might lead to prejudice or privilege.

The legal scholar Kimberlé Crenshaw first used the term "intersectionality" in the late 1980s. It originated as a response to the marginalization of Black women within the feminist and anti-racist movements. Since then, the concept of intersectionality has emerged as an indispensable theoretical lens through which to examine the multiplicity of oppressions experienced by members of socially excluded groups.

Societal Implications Recognizing and resolving the unique issues experienced by individuals with intersecting identities is emphasized by the concept of intersectionality. There is a call to action for campaigning and policymaking that takes into account the myriad perspectives of historically oppressed groups. Societies can advance social justice and eliminate systematic disparities by adopting the intersectionality framework.

Thirdly, Stereotypes of Men and Women, Dispelling the Myths and Expectations

Gender stereotypes are commonly held ideas about what it means to be a certain gender, including the duties, actions, and qualities that are expected of people. As a result, people are less likely to be able to freely and openly express their genuine gender identity, and these preconceptions are more likely to promote traditional norms and expectations.

Origins and Historical Context: Gender stereotypes have profound historical foundations, sustained by cultural, religious, and societal standards. Media, education, and socialization all play a role in perpetuating these stereotypes, which in turn shape people's ideas about what it means to be male or female and set unrealistic expectations for them.

Consequences for Society: Gender stereotypes help keep women at a disadvantage in society. They restrict one's professional options, control one's social life, and promote unhealthy ideas of physical attractiveness. Discrimination and prejudice against people of different gender identities are fueled by stereotypes, which has a negative impact on their ability to fully participate in society and thrive. In order to create more welcoming communities, it is crucial to combat these preconceived notions.

Conclusion

Our knowledge of gender dynamics and inequality relies heavily on the concepts of patriarchy, intersectionality, and gender stereotypes. To perpetuate systemic discrimination against women and other oppressed genders, patriarchy is a power structure that has historically favored men. The concept of intersectionality highlights the multiple forms of oppression that individuals encounter as a result of their identities and experiences. On the other hand, gender stereotypes restrict people's choices and chances based on false ideas about how people of different genders should behave.

It will need a group effort on the part of all of society to tackle these ideas. The path to a more equitable future can be paved by opposing patriarchal practices, embracing intersectionality, and breaking down gender stereotypes. Dismantling these oppressive structures requires education, awareness, and inclusive policies. The first steps in building a society in which every person, regardless of their gender identity or background, may thrive and contribute meaningfully are the acceptance of diversity, the validation of lived experiences, and the promotion of acceptance and understanding. Achieving true gender equality and social justice for all can be aided by such initiatives.

Chapter 2: Understanding the Roots of Gender Inequality

➢ Exploration of cultural and societal norms shaping gender roles

Introduction

Gender roles are mostly determined by cultural and societal conventions, which shape the ways in which people are expected to act, express themselves, and take part in society. Gender norms permeate all cultures, determining how individuals are expected to behave and what is expected of them. This essay delves into the cultural and social standards that determine gender roles, investigating their historical roots, contemporary expressions, and far-reaching consequences. With this knowledge, we may better grasp the nuances of gender relations and seek to create more equal and accepting communities.

One, the origins of gender norms in the past

The earliest examples of gender norms can be found in ancient communities, when men and women were assigned different responsibilities depending on their perceived skills. Biological differences generally determined who did what; for example, men were given jobs that required physical strength, while women were responsible for child care and housework. These early divisions of labor provided the foundation for gender stereotypes that remained through generations.

Norms for men and women have been shaped in large part by religious and cultural traditions and writings. Religious and cultural norms often prescribe distinct roles and responsibilities for men and women in terms of how they should act and what they should wear in public. These customs are typically passed down from generation to generation and are intricately linked to a people's sense of who they are as a people.

2. Cultural Expressions of Gender Norms
Various cultural practices There is a vast range of gender standards and expectations because of this. Some societies have very distinct roles for men and women, with little room for collaboration. Other cultures, on the other hand, accept a wider range of gender identities and expressions because of this.

The move from childhood to adulthood is marked by rites of passage in many cultures. Instilling the social obligations and privileges that come with being a man or a woman, these rituals frequently reinforce existing gender stereotypes. The flexibility of individuals to explore their gender identity might be constrained by rites of passage that reinforce stereotypical gender roles.

Third, the Effects of Gender Roles on People and Societies
Socialization: Children are taught gender roles by their parents, teachers, and peers from an early age. Children are socialized to develop gender-typical habits, interests, and abilities. This

kind of upbringing only serves to perpetuate rigid gender norms and stifle individual development.

Opportunities in the Workplace Gender roles have a major impact on workplace conditions. Many cultures have norms in place that restrict women from pursuing specific fields of work or pay them less than males for equal effort. Women's economic empowerment is hindered by a lack of education and work possibilities, which in turn reinforces gender inequity. Men, too, are subject to societal pressure to conform to certain expectations regarding their employment paths.

Health and Well-being: Gender norms influence health outcomes and access to healthcare services. Examples include how society often regulates and scrutinizes women's reproductive health. In addition, men may be less likely to seek medical attention for health problems due to rigid masculine ideals, which can delay diagnosis and treatment. The health of individuals and communities is compromised by these gendered restrictions.

4. Contemporary shifts in gender roles

More people are aware of the negative effects of strictly enforced gender standards thanks to feminist movements and lobbying activities. Groups and individuals working for social change are arguing for more equitable policies and practices, including the elimination of discrimination based on gender. These actions are made with the intention of eliminating discriminatory standards and allowing for a wider range of gender identities and manifestations.

The media significantly contributes to the formation of society norms and conceptions of gender by the representations it presents. The media's positive portrayal of several gender identities has the potential to dismantle prejudice and improve people's awareness of gender issues. However, media can also promote detrimental standards by reinforcing traditional gender roles and presenting stereotypes in an uncritical manner. Efforts to promote gender-sensitive media portrayal are vital in influencing society perceptions.

Gender norms can be challenged and changed via empowerment and education. Teaching students about different gender identities, combating stereotyping, and encouraging critical thinking are all important ways in which schools and other educational institutions may help advance gender equality. By giving people the tools they need to succeed, we give them the confidence to challenge established conventions and become agents of change in their communities.

Conclusion
Daily, people's lives and communities are impacted by the cultural and societal standards that shape gender roles. In order to combat gender inequality and promote more welcoming cultures, it is crucial to get an understanding of the origins, manifestations, and effects of these norms. Individuals can live in communities where they are safe to be themselves regarding their gender identification and where they are supported in pursuing their goals without having to worry about how others would react.

Acceptance of a wide range of gender identities and expressions strengthens communities and promotes peace and prosperity. Every person, organization, and institution must do their part to eradicate discrimination based on gender and usher in a day where all people are treated equally. Together, we can create a more just and inclusive world where people of all genders have the freedom to be themselves without the shackles of traditional gender norms.

➢ Analysis of the impact of media and popular culture on gender perceptions

The ideas, values, and norms of a society are shaped in large part by the media and popular culture. These powerful online communities play a major role in shaping gender roles, prejudices, and expectations. Examining the ways in which various media portrayals of men and women either uphold or subvert stereotypical gender norms, this essay dives deeply into the complicated relationship between media, popular culture, and gender attitudes. Understanding the larger implications for gender equality and cultural views on gender can be gleaned by analyzing the impact of media and popular culture.

1. Gender Stereotypes and Their Representation in the Media

Media representations: programs and films frequently reinforce gender stereotypes by casting men and women in narrow, fixed roles. Traditional conceptions of femininity are reinforced when women are portrayed as too emotional, dependent, or hypersexualized. In contrast, stereotypical portrayals of men tend to portray them as aggressive, domineering, and emotionless. These representations not only affect how people think about gender, but also how they act and what they anticipate from others.

Unrealistic beauty standards promoted by advertisements are a major cause of body dissatisfaction and low self-esteem, especially among women and young girls. There is a correlation between unrealistic media ideals of beauty and the development of eating disorders and other negative health outcomes, particularly among young people. The objectification of women's bodies in advertising further perpetuates detrimental gender stereotypes, turning women to simple commodities for purchase.

2. How Gender Norms Are Reinforced in Popular Culture
Lyrics in popular music frequently feature sexist and objectifying references to women, making it a potent source of cultural reinforcement. Harmful gender stereotypes are reinforced by songs that celebrate male superiority, the objectification of women, and toxic masculinity. Lyrics like these not only reflect but also normalize preexisting social standards, influencing listeners' views on gender roles and romantic partnerships.

Gender Roles in Video Games: A Major Aspect of Modern Pop Culture Many popular video games stereotype women as helpless victims or sexual objects, while men are shown as strong heroes. Traditional gender stereotypes are reinforced by the lack of strong, diverse female characters and by the prominence of clichéd portrayals. Players' perceptions and assumptions may be shaped by these images, contributing to a culture of sexism in the gaming industry and beyond.

3. How the Media and Pop Culture Affect How We Socialize
Children and teenagers are especially susceptible to media manipulation because of their open minds and open hearts. Young children's early exposure to gendered media can have lasting effects on their development, including the

reinforcement of stereotypes and the suppression of open-minded exploration of gender differences. Internalizing gender standards through media-driven indoctrination impacts young people's self- and social-perception, which in turn shapes their relationships and life goals.

While social media platforms can be great places for hearing new perspectives, they also have the potential to reinforce existing gender norms and stereotypes. Many public figures, both influential and otherwise, present carefully crafted images that uphold stereotypical notions of gender. Pressure to adhere to gender standards in one's online persona and interactions can be amplified on social media sites.

4 Media Literacy and Challenging Stereotypes about Women

Education about the media is important because it gives people the tools they need to evaluate and question what they see in the news and other forms of media. By learning how to identify biased content and critically engage with media messages, people can be empowered to confront inaccurate portrayals and harmful prejudices. Making people more critical consumers of media requires teaching them how to spot propaganda and the effects of stereotypical gender roles in visuals.

It is the obligation of media makers, advertisers, and content providers to encourage inclusive and diverse representations that challenge traditional gender standards. A more diverse and inclusive media landscape can be achieved by the increased representation of strong, complex female characters, positive portrayals of LGBTQ+ individuals, and nuanced views of masculinity. A more inclusive culture can be fostered through the promotion and support of content that challenges normative gender roles.

Conclusion

There are several ways in which media and pop culture shape how we think about gender. Media portrayals contribute to the maintenance of gender inequality and discrimination by reinforcing old gender norms and stereotypes. From television shows and movies to advertising, music, and video games, the influence of media permeates into every facet of society, affecting individuals' views and attitudes.

The media's influence, however, extends far beyond the simple repetition of negative perceptions. To combat damaging gender norms, it is crucial to teach media literacy, analyze media content critically, and advocate for diverse portrayals in the media. Societies can strive toward demolishing damaging gender preconceptions and building a more fair and inclusive environment for all persons, regardless of gender identity, by questioning the existing quo, pushing for diverse and authentic portrayals, and developing media literacy. One's ability to shape the future in which gender equality is not just a goal but a lived reality for all people depends in large part on the media's willingness to embrace diversity and question traditional gender stereotypes.

➤ Examination of religious and traditional beliefs influencing gender discrimination

Religious and traditional ideas have long been powerful forces in molding societal norms, values, and actions. However, these ideas have also been exploited to explain and sustain gender inequality, despite their potential for good. The interconnected nature of religious teachings, traditional beliefs, and prejudice against women is the focus of this article. These beliefs' intricate interplay with religion, tradition, and gender discrimination can be better understood by investigating their historical roots, contemporary interpretations, and contemporary effects.

1. Gender Roles in Religious Texts

Faith and behavior in religious communities are frequently based on interpretations and historical contexts of religious texts. However, there is considerable room for interpretation within these writings, and hence for a wide range of perspectives on appropriate gender roles. Some readings place an emphasis on mutual respect and esteem between the sexes, while others uphold a patriarchal order in which men are superior to women and the latter must submit to their authority. These interpretations, in turn, shape how religious teachings are understood and applied in society, which in turn is shaped by historical and cultural settings.

Effects on Women: Some faiths' teachings provide a moral justification for the suppression of women's freedoms and agency. Religion is frequently cited as a justification for limiting women's freedom of expression, movement, and dress. These restrictions reinforce old gender norms and impede women's social, economic, and political empowerment, therefore perpetuating gender inequality.

2. Gender Discrimination and the Role of Traditional Practices
Rites & Rituals: Traditional traditions, deeply established in cultural heritage, can reinforce gender discrimination through rituals and ceremonies. Female genital mutilation, child marriage, and honor killings are all practices that are commonly defended by appealing to cultural norms and customs. In addition to promoting gender inequality, these destructive practices have serious and lasting effects on women and girls' bodies, minds, and spirits.

Traditional values typically provide distinct roles and responsibilities for men and women within households and communities. Traditionally, men have taken on the roles of breadwinners and decision-makers, while women have been relegated to the home front. Individuals' capacity to express their gender identity and pursue their goals is curtailed as a result of these societal norms, perpetuating discrimination and inequity.

Third, difficulties and changes in interpretation
Feminist theology is a rising trend within religious traditions that aims to reinterpret sacred texts and practices with an eye toward how they apply to women and other marginalized groups. Proponents of equality and justice within religious communities, feminist theologians critique patriarchal

interpretations. Their efforts have paved the way for readings of the Bible that are more gender neutral and affirm the value and worth of all people.

Interfaith Dialogue: Interfaith dialogue provides a venue for varied religious communities to engage in debates concerning gender equality and prejudice. Interfaith discussion may combat narrow views and advance a more inclusive understanding of gender in religious contexts by bringing together religious leaders, scholars, and practitioners in open conversation. It promotes working together across denominational lines to achieve goals like increasing access to education and enhancing the status of women.

4. Effects on LGBTQ+ Groups

To exclude and discriminate against those who identify as LGBTQ+, religious concepts and traditional beliefs are commonly employed. Exclusion, social stigma, and discrimination within religious communities are common results of the explicit condemnation of same-sex partnerships and gender non-conforming identities in many religious beliefs. Due to these interpretations, LGBTQ+ people may experience rejection from their family, religious communities, and wider society.

While these obstacles exist, there are progressive initiatives within many faiths that fight for LGBTQ+ equality and acceptance. Faith communities can do more to welcome and support LGBTQ+ people, and LGBTQ+ affirming religious communities and their allies are doing just that. They question prejudiced readings and highlight the importance of kindness, tolerance, and respect for all people, regardless of sexual orientation or gender identity.

Conclusion

Gender norms, like any other aspect of society, are heavily influenced by religious and traditional beliefs. Although these ideas have historically served to uphold sexist practices and bolster conservative values, they are not set in stone. Changing social ideals and conceptions of gender equality can lead to new ways of viewing religious texts and practices.

Multifaceted strategies are needed to combat gender discrimination in the setting of deeply held religious and cultural views. Engaging in interfaith discussion, advancing feminist theology, and supporting LGBTQ+ affirming movements are crucial steps toward addressing discriminatory interpretations and establishing more inclusive religious communities. Individuals in religious environments need to be given the tools—through education, awareness, and advocacy—to question their own beliefs and stand up to discriminatory norms and attitudes.

Respect for religious freedom and promotion of fundamental human rights, especially gender equality, must be balanced in order to create a more inclusive and equitable society. Societies can strive toward eliminating discriminatory beliefs and practices, creating conditions where all people, regardless of gender or identity, can live with dignity, respect, and equality, by developing dialogue, understanding, and acceptance within religious and traditional frameworks. These initiatives have the potential to pave the way for a future where people of all faiths and backgrounds may find common ground on issues of equality, compassion, and respect for human rights.

➢ Case studies showcasing gender disparities in various cultures and regions

Gender inequities remain across the globe, manifesting in varied forms and intensities across different cultures and areas. These differences, which perpetuate gender inequality, have their origins in a variety of social, cultural, and historical factors. This essay delves into several different case studies from various areas and civilizations to illuminate the complex nature of gender inequality. By looking at these actual cases, we may better understand the difficulties women confront and the critical nature of eliminating gender inequality.

1.A Case Study of Educational Disparities between Men and Women in Afghanistan
Girls' and women's education is at risk in Afghanistan due to persistent gender gaps. Girls' access to education has been hindered by a number of factors, including cultural standards, security concerns, and economic difficulties. UNICEF reports that compared to boys, far fewer girls enroll in and complete elementary and secondary school. Due to cultural norms, girls are typically denied equal educational chances. To make matters worse, gender-based violence and cultural restrictions further limit girls' access to education, widening the gap between the sexes in terms of intelligence, employability, and economic prospects.

Second Case Study: The United States' Gender Pay Gap
Despite progress in women's rights, the wage disparity persists in the United States. The U.S. Census Bureau reports that

women, and women of color in particular, earn much less than men. This gap is caused by a confluence of variables, including occupational segregation, discrimination, and the absence of family-friendly workplace rules. Women are generally underrepresented in high-paying sectors and leadership roles, resulting to large wage differences over a lifetime. The gender pay gap is indicative of broader disparities and highlights the need for pay equity and workplace equality measures.

3 Case Analysis: Violence Against Women in India
Gender-based violence, such as intimate partner abuse, sexual harassment, and trafficking, has been a persistent problem in India. There is a hostile atmosphere for women because of entrenched patriarchal norms, cultural attitudes, and lax legal enforcement. There is an immediate need for comprehensive measures to address gender-based violence, as occurrences like the infamous Nirbhaya case in Delhi show, notwithstanding legislative reforms. Although awareness has increased because to grassroots movements and advocacy efforts, there are still obstacles to overcoming when it comes to safeguarding the safety and security of women.

Many countries in Sub-Saharan Africa, the Middle East, and some areas of Asia continue to practice Female Genital Mutilation (FGM). Cultural norms on femininity, modesty, and marriageability are reflected in FGM. Girls and women suffer negative health, mental, and reproductive outcomes as a result of this practice. Traditional beliefs, cultural pressure, and a lack of education all contribute to the perpetuation of FGM despite international efforts and legislation against cutting. This highlights the difficulty in overcoming deeply rooted gender inequality.

Japan as a Case Study in Inadequate Representation in Politics
The representation of women in politics remains a major issue in Japan. Low numbers of women in leadership roles can be seen in both the public and private spheres, reflecting the gender gap in political engagement. Cultural norms emphasizing women's duty as caregivers can discourage them from entering politics. Gender gaps in political representation persist despite growing efforts to encourage women to run for office, reflecting broader societal conventions and views about women in positions of authority.

Chapter 3: Intersectionality: Overlapping Identities and Inequalities

➢ Definition and significance of intersectionality in the context of gender equality

In recent years, the critical framework of intersectionality has emerged as a central topic in debates over sexism and racism. Coined by Kimberlé Crenshaw, a law scholar and feminist activist, intersectionality underscores the linked nature of social identities and the overlapping systems of oppression and discrimination that individuals may endure. An awareness of how race, ethnicity, class, sexual orientation, disability, and other dimensions of identity overlap and interact with gender is crucial for advancing the cause of gender equality. This essay discusses what intersectionality is, why it matters, and what it means for the fight for gender parity.

1. Intersectionality: A Multi-Faceted Perspective .
Intersectionality is the understanding that people are members of numerous social groups at once, and that the intersections between these groups affect how people are privileged or oppressed. By highlighting the interconnection of multiple forms of discrimination, it poses a challenge to the conventional binary approach to studying social issues.

Each person's identity is complex and has many facets; it can't be reduced to a single factor. The ways in which women of different races, sexual orientations, financial backgrounds, or physical or mental abilities encounter discrimination are just a few examples. Intersectionality is the recognition that marginalization is experienced in a variety of ways due to the complex interplay of multiple identities.

Intersectionality's Role in Promoting Gender Equality
Intersectionality broadens our knowledge of feminism by valuing women's varied life experiences. It makes sure that the experiences of women from underrepresented groups are taken into account by feminism rather than being ignored or written off as irrelevant. Women of color, LGBTQ+ women, disabled women, and low-income women all face distinct obstacles in today's society, and intersectional feminism seeks to alleviate those problems.

Intersectionality illuminates the tangled nature of power structures and the mutual reinforcement of oppressive systems. For instance, a woman of color may be subjected to multiple forms of discrimination at once, including racism, sexism, and classism, resulting in a complex collection of difficulties that cannot be solved by focusing on just one of them alone. A more sophisticated comprehension of the power dynamics at play can be uncovered with the use of intersectional analysis, which helps to reveal these relationships.

Intersectionality has far-reaching consequences for both policy and advocacy work. It highlights the necessity for tailor-made policy solutions that take into account the complex identities of individuals. Recognizing and amplifying the voices of underrepresented communities increases the efficacy of advocacy movements as well. By recognizing the intersecting forms of prejudice, advocates may campaign for policies that are truly inclusive and equitable.

3. Intersectionality's Difficulties and Critiques

Intersectionality is difficult because of its richness and nuance. Complex interactions between causes and their effects on specific people call for detailed analysis. Opponents of intersectionality point out that the concept is vague and hard to measure systematically, which hampers its usefulness in some settings.

Intersectionality highlights the significance of inclusiveness, although actual inclusiveness within advocacy movements and policymaking can be difficult to achieve. Constant work to remove barriers and raise up underrepresented voices is necessary to ensure that people from all walks of life are heard and understood.

4 Case Studies of Intersectionality in Practice

Empowerment at Work: Intersectionality sheds emphasis on the economic inequalities that women from different origins experience. For example, women of color often encounter wage inequalities that are greater than those experienced by white women. Policies that take into account these overlapping elements, such as race and gender, are necessary to address economic inequities and establish tailored interventions that uplift vulnerable communities.

Intersectionality is key to comprehending healthcare inequalities. Higher rates of assault, discrimination, and insufficient access to healthcare are experienced by women from marginalized populations, such as transgender women of color. Healthcare policies can better meet the needs of people who experience intersections of gender identity, race, and sexual orientation if we acknowledge these complexities.

5. Insights into the Future: Intersectionality and the Promotion of Gender Equality

By recognizing the multiplicity and interconnectedness of human experiences, the intersectionality paradigm strengthens our grasp of gender parity. Intersectionality offers a more nuanced understanding of gender inequalities by taking into account the different tiers of privilege and oppression that individuals may experience. It encourages us to examine the ways in which our identities and contexts interact and impact our experiences, which in turn strengthens our capacity for compassion, acceptance, and unity across our many groups.

Policymaking, lobbying, and social movements must all incorporate intersectionality if they are to be effective in promoting gender equality. By promoting inclusivity, amplifying minority voices, and tackling the interlocking forms of prejudice, societies may create a more fair future for all individuals, regardless of their identities. Intersectionality encourages us to see the worth and dignity in all people, to value their individual perspectives, and to tear down the structures that keep inequity alive. A more just and equitable world for all can be achieved if the fight for gender equality expands to include all marginalized groups.

➢ Exploration of how race, class, sexuality, and other factors intersect with gender

It's not easy to get a handle on gender without thinking about how other identities, such as race, class, sexual orientation, and ethnicity, connect with it. These factors do not act independently, but rather interact with one another to form the totality of an individual's chances and problems. This essay delves into the complex ways in which race, class, sexual orientation, and other identities interact with gender. The importance of taking a holistic view of social justice and equality is underscored by the insights gained from exploring these points of contact.

Social standards, power dynamics, and opportunities have all been influenced by the interplay of races and sexes throughout history. For instance, women of color have traditionally experienced multiple forms of discrimination that stem from the combination of racism and sexism. Access to school, employment, and social services has been molded by both racial and gendered biases, which has a disproportionate impact on Black women, Indigenous women, and women from other marginalized racial origins.

The concept of "double jeopardy," when members of historically oppressed racial and gender groups experience double discrimination, is illuminated by the study of intersectionality. It is critical, however, to honor the strength and resiliency already present in these neighborhoods. Women of color have been at the vanguard of social justice movements for decades, fighting for racial and gender equality even as they face numerous forms of oppression.

2. Disparities in Wealth by Class and Gender
Access to resources, education, and career prospects are unequal for people of different socioeconomic backgrounds and sexes. Economic mobility is hampered because women from lower socioeconomic origins have a harder time gaining access to excellent education and healthcare. Gender disparity in the workplace is exacerbated when working-class women face sexism in the workplace and less opportunities for growth.

Advocacy and Self-Sufficiency Intersectionality also draws attention to the tenacity and activism found in working-class neighborhoods. Women from the working class have always played an integral role in labor movements, fighting for equal pay and safer working conditions. The nexus of class and gender inequality must be addressed, and we can only do so by listening to and amplifying the voices of working-class women.

The Sexual Orientation and Gender Identity Spectrum
Wide Range of Sexual Orientations The many ways in which gender and sexuality intersect attest to the variety of sexual orientations that exist. Non-heterosexual and non-cisgender identities, such as lesbian, gay, bisexual, transgender, queer, and others, pose a challenge to conventional ideas of what it means to be a certain gender and sexuality. Discrimination, social stigma, and a lack of legal protections are only some of the issues that arise as a result of these overlapping identities.

The LGBTQ+ community has long been a leader in the fight for full sexual and gender equality. The concept of "intersectionality" in the LGBTQ+ community highlights the unique challenges faced by those who hold many identities. For example, transgender women of color encounter disproportionately high rates of assault and discrimination, underlining the significance of tackling both racial and gender disparities within LGBTQ+ advocacy initiatives.

4 Complex Intersections of Cultural and Religious Factors
Cultural Norms Cultural and religious ideas influence society and family norms and expectations through their intersection with gender. Conservative readings of religious texts and adherence to traditional gender norms might serve to perpetuate patriarchal attitudes and limit the agency of women and transgender people. Honor murders, female genital mutilation, and forced marriages are all examples of cultural practices that emphasize the linkages between culture, religion, and sexism.

There has been a shift within feminism toward an appreciation of cultural nuance, which acknowledges the enormous range of women's experiences around the globe. Advocacy for gender equality, according to intersectional feminism, must be culturally sensitive and inclusive, giving due weight to the unique experiences and viewpoints of women from a variety of backgrounds and traditions. It promotes the elimination of oppressive cultural norms and the elevation of women from all walks of life.

Insights Towards Inclusive Equality, Final Thoughts

Understanding the complexities of people's lives and struggles requires looking at how ethnicity, class, sexual orientation, and other characteristics intersect with gender. Embracing intersectionality is vital for developing a more inclusive and equitable society. Advocating for policies that address intersecting inequities and elevating the voices of marginalized populations are necessary steps in this direction.

Societies can work toward eliminating structural barriers and fostering genuine equality and justice for all members by acknowledging the interconnectivity of diverse social identities. An approach to social justice that is really inclusive values the uniqueness of each person and works to increase mutual respect, tolerance, and friendship among people of all walks of life. All people, regardless of their ethnicity, socioeconomic status, sexual orientation, or gender identity, need to be treated with respect and given equal opportunities in life.

➢ Real-life examples illustrating the complexities of intersectional discrimination

Multifaceted in nature, intersectional discrimination arises when an individual experiences bias on account of more than one social identity, such as race, gender, sexual orientation, socioeconomic status, or physical or mental impairment. These multiple identities make for rich and nuanced lived experiences, but they can also increase vulnerability to prejudice. This essay looks at real-life scenarios to demonstrate the complexities of intersectional discrimination, illuminating the difficulties individuals encounter when coping with numerous forms of oppression and stressing the critical need for systemic reform.

Disparities in Health Care for Black Women: A Case Study
When it comes to medical care, black women in the United States often face multiple forms of prejudice. Pregnancy outcomes are negatively impacted by the intersection of race and gender. Research shows that Black women had a higher risk of death or serious problems after childbirth compared to white women. This intersectional discrimination is the result of racial biases, limited healthcare access, and gendered preconceptions, and it shows how these identities interact to affect people's health and their ability to get the help they need.

LGBTQ+ Youth Homelessness: A Case Study

LGBTQ+ youth, especially those of color, face disproportionate rates of homelessness due to the intersection of their sexual orientation, gender identity, and race. Many LGBTQ+ youth become homeless as a result of discrimination and rejection at home and from wider society. The lack of security in homeless shelters for LGBTQ+ youth is a major issue. This case illustrates how the difficulties faced by people who are marginalized due to their sexual orientation, gender identity, and/or race overlap, putting them at increased risk of discrimination and homelessness.

3: A Case Study of Violence Against Indigenous Women
High rates of violence are experienced by indigenous women worldwide because of their gender, ethnicity, and socioeconomic condition. For Indigenous women, a hostile environment has been created by the intersection of historical colonization, systematic racism, and gender-based violence. Particularly high incidence of sexual assault, physical assault, and homicide are experienced by Indigenous women and girls in Canada. They are especially vulnerable due to the convergence of multiple forms of oppression, such as their gender, race, and socioeconomic background.

Disabled people, especially those who are members of historically oppressed racial or gender groups, endure prejudice on the job. Disabilities, racism, and sexism all compound each other to create even more obstacles for people trying to find work. Exclusion from the labor force is a result of the intersection of racial and gendered prejudices with disability-related stigmas and stereotypes. Professional advancement opportunities for these people may be hampered by barriers to education, training, and reasonable accommodations. Disabled people's career opportunities and economic mobility are severely hampered by this kind of intersectional discrimination.

5. A Case Study of Religious Discrimination Against Muslim Women

Muslim women often experience Islamophobia and sexism at the same time, which is an example of intersectional discrimination. Particularly vulnerable to religious prejudice and gender stereotypes are Muslim women who choose to wear the hijab. Because of their religious beliefs and the way they express their gender, they may be denied access to housing, public accommodations, and educational opportunities. This type of discrimination is emblematic of the difficulties Muslim women experience and highlights the need to combat biases based on both religion and gender simultaneously.

Conclusion

These real-world scenarios show how complex and destructive the effects of discrimination at multiple intersections can be. These stories indicate that individuals are not discriminated against based on a single component of their identity; instead, they confront compounded forms of bias due to the junction of various social circumstances. Comprehensive societal changes are needed to address intersectional discrimination, such as legislative reforms, educational initiatives, and cultural adjustments that combat prejudice and foster acceptance.

Intersectional discrimination is complex, but understanding it can help society create more sophisticated and effective tactics to oppose discrimination and advance social justice. Advocacy work, policy reforms, and public awareness campaigns must use an intersectional perspective to address the specific difficulties experienced by those on the margins of society. Societies can only build spaces where all members, regardless of their intersecting identities, can flourish, make valuable contributions, and live free from discrimination if they commit collectively to eliminating all forms of discrimination.

➢ Strategies for addressing intersectional inequalities and promoting inclusivity

The concept of intersectionality highlights the need for focused methods to alleviate disparities and develop inclusivity by highlighting the distinct types of discrimination that are created when social identities cross. The promotion of social justice in a world distinguished by a wide range of identities, experiences, and difficulties calls for all-encompassing strategies that take into account the nuances of intersectional discrimination. The necessity of recognizing and appreciating variety in all its manifestations is emphasized, and methods for resolving intersectional disparities and promoting inclusivity across many fields are discussed in this essay.

Improving Educational Practices for All Students
Diversifying school curricula is a vital strategy for tackling intersectional disparities. Having textbook authors and contributors represent a wide range of identities and life experiences promotes a more welcoming classroom setting. Students who are exposed to several worldviews grow in their capacity for compassion, understanding, and acceptance of others.

Inclusive Policies: Educational institutions should develop inclusive policies that accommodate to the different requirements of students. This involves addressing racial inequities in disciplinary procedures, creating LGBTQ+ support groups, and helping students with impairments. Students from all walks of life benefit from inclusive policies because they help everyone feel welcome and safe in the classroom.

Training for teachers and other school personnel in intersectionality and cultural sensitivity is an important part of professional development. Teachers may better create classrooms where all children feel valued and supported when they participate in professional development programs that highlight the importance of knowing multiple identities, confronting biases, and building inclusive classrooms.

Promoting Diversity and Inclusion in the Workplace .
Organizations can combat intersectional inequities by embracing diverse hiring practices. This means making an effort to hire people from a wide range of backgrounds, advocating for the inclusion of traditionally underrepresented groups, and addressing biases in the selection process. Teams with a wide range of backgrounds and experiences are more likely to generate novel solutions to problems.

Organizations should make it a top priority to increase diversity among their executives. This involves promoting the professional advancement of persons from underrepresented communities, providing mentorship programs, and offering leadership training adapted to the unique issues faced by disadvantaged individuals. Having more people from different backgrounds in positions of power is important for making fair and inclusive decisions.

Flexible working hours, parental leave, and access to low-cost health care are all examples of equitable workplace rules that can help foster a more welcoming environment for all employees. Policies like these are designed to help employees of all backgrounds and abilities thrive in the workplace. A workplace that values diversity and inclusion in its perks creates a more welcoming and productive space for all employees.

3.Reforms to the Law to Guarantee Equal Protection
Laws against discrimination should be made more stringently enforced in order to help reduce intersectional inequities. Discrimination on the basis of race, gender, sexual orientation, gender identity, disability, or any other element that intersects with these should be expressly forbidden by law. To further guarantee the safety of vulnerable populations, legal systems must adapt to new ways of thinking about issues like identification and discrimination.

Racial Disparities In The Criminal Justice System, Employment, Education, And Healthcare Should Be Targeted By Legislative Reforms. Policies that focus on eliminating systematic racism, fostering racial equity, and addressing the core causes of racial inequities are vital for achieving a just society.

4. Representation in the Media: Challenging Stereotypes and Fostering Acceptance
Fair and accurate portrayals: media outlets have a powerful impact on public opinion. It's crucial that more people of different backgrounds and experiences be shown on screen, in

commercials, and in the news. By exposing people to multiple perspectives, we can break down prejudices and encourage tolerance and acceptance.

Storytellers have a responsibility to critically examine the messages they convey via their work. Storytellers have a responsibility to avoid stereotyping, portray marginalized groups fairly, and solicit feedback from those in those groups to guarantee authenticity and cultural sensitivity in their work. Promoting diverse communities and eliminating discriminatory narratives are two outcomes of ethical media portrayal.

5. Community Engagement: Allyship and the Construction of Inclusive Spaces

Dialogue in the Community: It is crucial to encourage communities to have honest and civil discussions about complex intersectional concerns. Community conversations encourage people to open up to one another, question their biases, and discover new things. Workshops, seminars, and awareness drives all serve to open up channels of communication and mutual comprehension.

In order to combat intersectional inequities, it is important to encourage allies to step up. Supporting and campaigning for oppressed populations is an example of allyship on the part of those from more advantaged backgrounds. To combat discriminatory attitudes and actions and promote more welcoming policies, allies can utilize their positions of power to magnify the voices of those they support. Promoting allyship creates solidarity and strengthens the collaborative endeavor toward social justice.

6. Educational Initiatives: Promoting Understanding and Combating Prejudice

Public Awareness Campaigns: Educational campaigns that focus on intersectionality, diversity, and inclusion are strong instruments for addressing biases and developing understanding. Social media, television, and local events are all viable venues for such initiatives, which aim to reach a wide audience and dispel damaging misconceptions.

Training programs that encourage cultural competence and intersectional awareness should be extensively adopted. Schools, businesses, the police, hospitals, and other institutions can all benefit from programs that teach participants to recognize and overcome their own prejudices while also learning to appreciate those of others.

Conclusion

Recognizing the intricacies of many identities and experiences is essential for tackling intersectional injustices and fostering a culture of inclusion. Societies can create environments where people from all walks of life are valued, respected, and given equal opportunities by enacting educational reforms, fostering workplace inclusivity, enacting legal protections, promoting diverse media representation, engaging communities, and conducting educational campaigns.

As opposed to merely acknowledging diversity, intersectionality promotes empathy and the elimination of institutionalized forms of discrimination. These methods help societies get closer to their ideal of creating just and fair communities in which people of all identities and backgrounds can flourish, make valuable contributions, and enjoy a life free from discrimination. By working together to eliminate intersectional disparities, we can create a world where everyone's perspectives and experiences are acknowledged and valued.

Chapter 4: Women's Empowerment and Economic Justice

➤ Overview of economic disparities between genders

Economic inequality between the sexes is nothing new, and it reflects long-standing social conventions and biases. Despite tremendous advances in many areas of gender equality, economic discrepancies exist between men and women. This article presents an overview of the economic gaps between the sexes, including their sources, effects, and proposed remedies.

1. The Persistent Difference in Pay Between Men and Women
The wage gap is the discrepancy between men's and women's wages in the job market. Women around the world, on average, earn less than men for equal or comparable labor, regardless of their education and professional background.

Causes: Several factors contribute to the gender wage gap, including occupational segregation, where women are concentrated in lower-paying sectors; discrimination and prejudices in hiring, promotions, and compensation negotiations; and the undervaluation of traditionally female-dominated professions. Women's long-term earning power is negatively affected by professional breaks brought on by caring for children and other family members.

2 Gender Gaps in Business and Management

In the business world, women frequently face more obstacles than men when trying to launch or grow their own companies due to a lack of resources and support. Persistent economic disparities in the business world are exacerbated by the fact that women entrepreneurs continue to face bias in investment decisions and loan approvals.

Although women have made great strides in recent decades, they are still vastly outnumbered by males in positions of power in business, government, and academia. There is a significant gender gap in leadership roles because of barriers such as the glass ceiling and unconscious bias.

3 Disparities between Men and Women in the Labor Force and the Informal Economy
Unemployment: In times of economic hardship, women are hit harder than males by the job market. Higher unemployment rates among women can be attributed to structural issues including discrimination and restricted access to education and occupational training.

Women are disproportionately represented in informal labor sectors, which often have lower earnings, less job security, and fewer benefits for their workers than official ones. Women are particularly vulnerable to exploitation and economic insecurity due to the absence of legal safeguards they enjoy when working in informal labor.

4 The Effect of Gender Inequality in Economic Conditions on Women's Happiness

Economic inequality contributes to increased poverty rates among women, especially single moms and female-headed households. Women and their families suffer when they cannot afford basic necessities like an education, medical care, and healthy food.

Violence against women because of economic dependence on partners or family members. They can't break free of the cycle of violence and instability because they lack the resources to do so.

5 Interventions and Policy Efforts
Equal Pay Legislation: Implementing and implementing equal pay legislation is vital for lowering the gender wage gap. Equal pay for equal work is a fundamental human right, and governments and organizations have a responsibility to eliminate discrimination in the workplace.

Quotas and Affirmative Action Quotas and affirmative action measures can increase the number of women in positions of power. These steps are crucial in ending the history of male dominance in positions of power and creating more welcoming environments at work.

Investing in women's education and training improves their economic prospects by increasing their access to higher education, vocational training, and programs that help them acquire and hone new skills. When money is put toward the education of girls and programs in STEM (science, technology, engineering, and mathematics), it opens doors for women to enter male-dominated fields that pay well.

In order to help women start and grow businesses, it is important to provide them with resources such as funding, mentorship programs, and opportunities to connect with other businesswomen. To level the playing field for businesses managed by women, financial institutions and investors should work to eliminate gender biases in funding decisions.

Conclusion

Persistent gender economic gaps are a major obstacle to achieving equality and social justice. It will take a diverse strategy, including changes to the law, public education campaigns, and sector-specific measures, to reduce these inequalities. The hurdles that keep countries from eliminating economic inequalities can be broken down by enacting laws that encourage equal pay, boost women's representation in leadership roles, invest in education and training, and assist women entrepreneurs.

Gender prejudices and stereotypes can't be eradicated alone by legislative action; cultural and societal attitudes must also change. Providing women with economic opportunities has a multiplicative effect on society and the economy at large. Through coordinated efforts at the individual, societal, and institutional levels, societies can establish conditions where men and women have equal opportunities, enabling them to contribute fully to the economy and society as a whole. Together, we can create a world where gender-based economic inequities are a thing of the past, paving the way for a more just and inclusive future.

➢ Analysis of workplace discrimination and the gender pay gap

Discrimination against women in the workplace and the gender pay gap are two examples of the established biases and inequities that remain in communities around the world. The gender pay gap is a glaring illustration of the prejudice that women still experience in the workplace, even after decades of progress in women's rights and gender equality movements. This essay examines the causes, effects, and potential remedies of discrimination in the workplace and the gender wage gap.

Discrimination in the Workplace: Its Many Faces and Repercussions

Discrimination against women in the workplace can manifest itself in a number of ways, such as salary disparity, a lack of promotion possibilities, the perpetuation of harmful stereotypes based on gender, harassment, and unfair hiring and promotion policies. Microaggressions, exclusionary actions, and structural prejudices inside institutions are all examples of more covert forms of discrimination.

Women's health, career advancement opportunities, and job happiness are all negatively impacted by prejudice in the workplace. Women who have been subjected to discrimination often suffer from low self-esteem, increased stress, and a feeling of isolation. They are unable to advance in their careers due to discrimination, which has a negative impact on their earning potential and leadership opportunities. Mental health problems, lower productivity at work, and a loss of morale are all possible outcomes of discrimination in the workplace.

The Gender Pay Gap: Roots and Repercussions

The Real Reasons Why Women Make Less Money: Occupational segregation, in which women are more likely to work in lower-paying fields, discrimination in salary negotiations and promotions, a dearth of family-friendly workplace policies, and the undervaluing of traditionally female-dominated professions all contribute to the gender pay gap. The motherhood penalty, in which women are punished for requesting flexible work arrangements or taking time off to care for children, also contributes to the wage disparity between men and women.

Women, especially those who are single moms, are disproportionately affected by poverty as a result of the gender wage gap. Long-term economic insecurity is the outcome because it prevents women from being financially independent, limits their access to education and healthcare, and affects their retirement savings. In addition, discrimination and inequality are entrenched due to the gender wage gap, which perpetuates detrimental gender stereotypes.

Discrimination and wage gaps are maintained by structural and cultural factors.

Biased hiring practices, a lack of diversity among company leaders, and a dearth of possibilities for mentoring and networking are all examples of structural barriers that contribute to the ongoing existence of prejudice in the workplace. Gender biases are typically engrained in business cultures, impeding women's advancement and contributing to unequal compensation and limited career options.

Discrimination in the workplace and the gender pay gap are exacerbated by entrenched cultural norms and traditional gender expectations. Hiring and promotion decisions are sometimes influenced by preconceived notions about women's ability, leadership potential, and dedication to their jobs. In order to eradicate sexist beliefs and advance gender parity, it is essential to tackle these cultural norms.

Reforms in Legislation and Policy
An essential first step in closing the gender wage gap is passing and enforcing strong equal pay legislation. Equal compensation for equal work must be mandated by law, and governments must take action to punish companies that practice discrimination. Accountability and fair pay can be encouraged via transparent salary regulations and reporting methods.

The gender pay gap can be closed by instituting family-friendly workplace policies like paid maternity leave, low-cost child care, and flexible scheduling. These measures help both men and women achieve a better work-life balance, with less repercussions for mothers who need to take time off to care for young children.

Women's Leadership Promotion: Increasing the number of women in organizational leadership roles is an important step in ending discrimination in the workplace. Gender quotas, affirmative action legislation, and mentorship programs can assist raise the proportion of women in decision-making roles, challenging existing biases and developing varied leadership styles.

5 Fostering Cultural Change via Education and Awareness
Awareness of discrimination and biases based on gender in the workplace can be increased through gender sensitization workshops. These initiatives need to reach out to management as well as workers in order to create an environment where everyone feels valued and safe.

The media's portrayal of an issue and its advocacy for it have a major impact on public opinion. Advocacy campaigns, positive media portrayals of women in a variety of roles, and the rejection of stereotypical assumptions can all change the way people think. The media may be a potent force for advancing gender parity and destroying discriminatory beliefs and practices.

Conclusion
Legal reforms, organizational rules, cultural shifts, and public awareness efforts are all necessary to close the gender pay gap and abolish discrimination in the workplace. Dismantling discriminatory practices and advancing gender equality in all facets of life requires concerted efforts from governments, employers, and civil society.

It is possible for cultures to establish conditions in which women are appreciated, respected, and afforded equal opportunity through the adoption of equal pay legislation, the promotion of family-friendly workplace practices, the encouragement of women in leadership roles, and the questioning of cultural norms and gender expectations. In order to create a more accepting and equal society, educational and awareness efforts are crucial.

Equal pay for equal work is a matter of economic fairness, but fighting discrimination in the workplace is a question of basic human rights. Women's empowerment in the workplace is good for people, families, businesses, and communities. It promotes workplaces that are more open to different perspectives and ideas and where employees of all genders feel valued and appreciated for their efforts. By working together in this way, societies can get themselves closer to true gender equality, where people of both sexes have the same opportunities for full participation, success, and advancement in society.

➢ Examination of women's entrepreneurship and financial inclusion

Promoting gender equality, empowering women, and driving economic growth, women's entrepreneurship and financial inclusion are critical elements of economic development. Despite tremendous advances in recent years, women, particularly in poor countries, sometimes face impediments to accessing financial resources and business opportunities. This essay looks at the barriers female business owners face, as well as the role financial inclusion plays in giving women more economic independence.

1. Obstacles Facing Female Entrepreneurs

One of the biggest obstacles that women business owners confront is a dearth of financial resources. Due to gender bias, a lack of collateral, or unfair lending policies, it can be difficult for women to obtain loans or venture capital. Because of this restriction, they are unable to launch or grow their enterprises.

Social pressures and preconceived notions about what women are and are not capable of doing can discourage them from starting their own businesses. Traditional gender roles may pressure women to prioritize home responsibilities above company initiatives, limiting their entrepreneurial pursuits. Women's self-belief and drive to succeed in business might be dampened by stereotypes and discrimination based on their gender.

Women company owners face a dearth of networking opportunities compared to their male colleagues, despite the fact that such interactions are essential to the development of any enterprise. Their ability to grow their businesses and improve their skills may be hampered by a lack of resources such as professional networks, mentors, and business support services.

Second, the significance of monetary participation
Financial independence is a major factor in a woman's economic independence. Female entrepreneurs, risk managers, and savers all benefit from equal access to banking, credit, and insurance products. Women who have more control over their financial lives often make larger contributions to family income and, by extension, to community growth.

Expanding company Opportunities: Women company owners benefit from increased access to capital thanks to greater financial inclusion. Women who have access to financing may find it easier to grow their businesses through investments in areas such as research and development, advertising, and staffing. Furthermore, financial services allow women business owners to enter official marketplaces, raising their profile and expanding their scope of possible customers.

To reduce poverty, especially among women, access to financial services is essential. Women in low-income communities can develop jobs and raise their families' level of life if they have access to microfinance services and cheap financing. The eradication of poverty and the advancement of society are aided greatly by women's economic independence Governments and policymakers can do a lot to help women become entrepreneurs and participate in the economy by enacting policy reforms. It is possible to create a more welcoming atmosphere for women business owners by enacting laws like gender-sensitive lending, financial literacy initiatives, and incentives for women-owned enterprises. Legal impediments should be removed, equal rights should be promoted, and women should be given equal access to financial services if policymakers are serious about ending prejudice.

Women can benefit greatly from a deeper comprehension of economic principles, investment strategies, and business administration by participation in specialized financial literacy classes. Women with higher levels of education are better able to handle the complexity of the financial system, run their businesses, and make sound financial judgments. Gaining financial literacy equips women to boldly advocate for their rights and secure their own financial futures.

Increasing Women's Access to Digital Financial Services New developments in technology, notably mobile banking and digital payment systems, offer the potential to greatly improve women's access to digital financial services. By eliminating the need to leave the house, the convenience of digital financial services helps women overcome geographical limitations in their pursuit of financial independence.

Conclusion

Entrepreneurial women and access to credit both contribute to economic growth and benefit society as a whole. Women's economic independence has a multiplicative influence on individuals, households, communities, and economies. Societies can unleash the potential of women entrepreneurs, boosting creativity, economic growth, and social development, by reducing barriers to women's entrepreneurship, expanding financial inclusion, and providing targeted support.

To help women business owners succeed at every turn, the government, banks, and nonprofits must work together to build a comprehensive ecosystem. Societies can prepare the way for a future where women are active participants in the entrepreneurial environment by promoting financial education, enacting supportive regulations, and using digital technology, thereby driving economic success and crafting a more fair society for all.

➢ Initiatives and policies promoting women's economic empowerment

The economic independence of women is not merely an issue of fairness; it is essential to long-term progress and broad prosperity. Since the importance of women's economic independence has been widely acknowledged, governments, international organizations, and civil society have all launched programs and policies to help women financially. Education, employment, entrepreneurship, financial inclusion, and legal reforms are just some of the areas where this essay focuses on initiatives and policies that empower women economically.

1.Programs to Improve Education and Professional Skills
Programs that help educate girls are among the best ways to help women gain economic independence. Societies can equip girls with the tools they need to succeed in higher education and in meaningful jobs if they provide them with equal access to great education. The cycle of poverty and illiteracy can be broken by programs like these that provide financial aid to families so that they can send their daughters to school.

Initiatives to get more women interested in studying STEM subjects are needed if they are to take part in the dynamic digital economy of the future. STEM education initiatives provide scholarships, mentorship programs, and workshops to push girls to seek STEM careers, reducing the gender gap in these high-demand fields and boosting innovation and entrepreneurship.

Adult education and training programs are extremely important for women, particularly those from underprivileged backgrounds. The goal of these programs is to empower women by teaching them marketable skills like as tailoring, craft making, and agricultural techniques so that they can support their families economically. Women's self-esteem and job prospects can both benefit from participation in skill-building programs.

2. Programs for Gainful Employment and the Workplace
The enforcement of equal opportunity employment regulations guarantees that women and men have equal access to employment, advancement, and compensation. Equal compensation, safe working environments, and a lack of harassment are just some of the ways in which governments and businesses may combat gender discrimination in the workplace. A more fair working environment can be fostered through open hiring and promotion procedures.

Employer-provided leave and other family-friendly benefits: Women are better able to juggle work and family life when their employers are accommodating to their needs in terms of scheduling, telecommuting, and parental leave. Family-friendly policies, including cheap childcare services, on-site daycare facilities, and lactation spaces, encourage working women, allowing them to remain in the workforce and pursue career growth.

Programs to Help Women Start Businesses Women-specific entrepreneurship support programs are commonly offered by governments and NGOs. Women can gain the confidence, knowledge, and tools to launch and expand their own businesses thanks to these programs' emphasis on mentoring, training, access to funding, and networking opportunities. Programs that encourage entrepreneurship equip women with the tools they need to start their own businesses, which boosts productivity and innovation.

Access to Financial Services and Other Supports
Small loans and other financial services are made available to women through microfinance banks and credit programs created especially for them, helping them to launch or grow enterprises, further their education, and provide for their families. Women's economic independence is fostered by microfinance programs, which give them the tools they need to take charge of their financial lives and make a positive impact on their households and communities.

To empower women economically, it is important to remove the impediments that prevent them from acquiring land and property. Women's access to capital for agriculture, housing, and businesses is hindered by a lack of legal protections and education about property rights, inheritance, and land tenure. Women's economic and financial security are improved when they have access to land and property.

Advocacy for Policy Changes and Changes to the Law
Reforms to the law that are sensitive to gender issues, such as those affecting inheritance and property rights and family law, are essential if we want to see more women gain economic

independence. Governments should implement and strictly enforce laws protecting women's rights to guarantee that they are afforded equal opportunities and are safe from harassment, abuse, and other forms of discrimination. Legal systems that take into account the needs of both sexes allow women to speak up for their rights and take an active role in the economy.

Policy Advocacy and Gender Mainstreaming: Civil society organizations and advocacy groups play a critical role in supporting women's economic empowerment through policy advocacy and gender mainstreaming activities. These groups help shape gender-inclusive policies and programs by campaigning for them, funding research on women's economic challenges, and spreading the word. In order to promote economic parity, it is important that the viewpoints and needs of women be taken into account in all areas of policymaking.

5 Expanding Opportunities for Women Entrepreneurs in New Markets

To promote economic growth and gender equality, it is critical to increase the number of women who start businesses in the technology and innovation industries. Innovation and entrepreneurship are bolstered by programs that help firms led by women to access resources including training, mentorship, and investment. Women's engagement in the knowledge-based economy can be improved by encouraging them to start businesses in fast-growing industries like artificial intelligence, biotechnology, and green technology.

The goal of social entrepreneurship is to create a profitable business that also helps people and the environment. Healthcare, education, environmental protection, and poverty reduction are just few of the areas that women-led social enterprises tackle. Supporting women social entrepreneurs empowers them to make positive social impact, promoting economic and cultural progress.

Chapter 5: Social Justice Movements and Policy Interventions

➢ Historical overview of feminist movements and their impact on society

Feminist movements have played a major role in creating civilizations across the globe, opposing centuries-old patriarchal norms, campaigning for women's rights, and driving social change. Feminist activists have diligently campaigned for gender equality, reproductive rights, employment equity, and an end to gender-based violence since the suffragette movements of the late 19th and early 20th centuries and continuing into the intersectional feminism of today. This article examines the development, major turning points, and far-reaching effects of feminist movements on society, culture, and legislation.

1. Early Feminism and the Struggle for Voting Rights
Feminism originated in Europe and North America in the late 19th and early 20th century. The suffragettes of this time were activists who fought for the right of women to vote. The campaign gained steam in the late 19th century, eventually leading to landmark triumphs like the suffrage movement in the UK and the 19th Amendment, which gave women the right to vote in the United States in 1920.

In questioning conventional gender roles and championing women's representation in politics, the first wave of feminism paved the way for subsequent movements. The Suffragettes opened the door for women to participate in politics and civic life, forever changing the landscape.

2. Second-Generation Feminism and the Fight for Equality between the Sexes

The second wave of feminism, which expanded its concerns beyond the right to vote, occurred in the 1960s and 1970s. Women's rights, job equality, and an end to discrimination and violence against women were some of the causes championed by activists at the time. Intersectionality of gender with other social elements such as ethnicity, class, and sexual orientation was also brought to light during the second wave.

Historic Moments: Title IX in the United States, which outlaws sex-based discrimination in education, was enacted during the second wave, as were women's studies programs and the emergence of women's liberation groups. Struggles for women's reproductive rights, such as abortion and contraception access, rose to prominence, changing discussions of women's bodily autonomy.

Critical Intersectionality and Third-Century Feminism

Rooted in the belief that social categories such as race, gender, and sexual orientation are inextricably intertwined, the third wave of feminism arose in the 1990s. This new group of feminists recognized the value of women's varied life experiences and worked to make the feminist movement more welcoming and accepting of all women.

Consequences: Third-wave feminism sparked debates on the value of diversity in identity and expression and opened the door to arguments about consent and gender fluidity. In addition, the movement embraced digital media, with activists all over the world networking online to increase their sense of solidarity and the volume of feminist voices. Furthermore, the special difficulties encountered by women of color, LGBTQ+ people, and other disadvantaged communities were brought to light by third wave feminism.

A digital presence and an emphasis on online action are hallmarks of the fourth wave of feminism, which arose in the 2010s. Feminists were able to effectively use social media to disseminate information, increase public understanding, and rally support for their goals. Since feminism is an international movement, the fourth wave also stressed international cooperation.

Highlights Sexual harassment (#MeToo movement), reproductive rights, and gender-based violence: all problems that received a boost in visibility because to online activism. To effect significant social change, fourth-wave feminists made use of hashtags, viral campaigns, and internet organizing. The movement also promoted discussions on issues like as toxic masculinity, consent education, and the value of allies.

5. Effects on Culture and Society

Laws have been changed to better promote gender equality, and feminist movements have been a major force in bringing about these changes. Legislation addressing domestic violence, sexual harassment, reproductive rights, and workplace discrimination has been affected by feminist agitation. Women now have more legal recourses and safety nets as a result of these reforms.

Cultural Shifts The emergence of feminist movements that questioned entrenched gender roles had a profound effect on society. There has been a shift toward more nuanced and inclusive conversations about consent, body image, and gender roles. Media portrayals of women have progressed, presenting a variety of stories and posing new questions about long-held preconceptions. Feminist campaigning has had an effect on society attitudes, as seen by the rising number of women in political and other leadership positions.

Problems and Possible Solutions
Although feminism has made great strides forward, there are still obstacles to overcome. There is still a worldwide impact on women from issues including gender-based violence, the wage gap, and lack of access to reproductive healthcare. Additionally, there is a need to promote greater diversity within the feminist movement, addressing the issues of women from varied backgrounds and experiences.

Feminist movement going ahead must maintain its focus on structural discrimination, push for legislative changes, and question accepted social mores. Important steps toward achieving the feminist agenda include acknowledging the importance of intersectionality, promoting global solidarity, and involving male supporters. Education, both official and informal, has a crucial role in fostering gender equality and combating prejudices from a young age.

Conclusion

The perseverance and resolve of female activists throughout history is reflected in the course of their movements. Feminists have made great strides, from suffrage to online activism, challenging conventional norms and systematic inequalities. The impact of these movements can be seen in the shape of legislative and cultural changes, as well as in the amplified volume of women's voices.

As civilizations continue to evolve, the necessity of feminism remains important. To make gender equality a reality for all people, regardless of their gender identity or background, feminists around the world must continue their work while also committing to intersectionality, inclusivity, and global solidarity. Feminist movements paved the way for a more equitable world, encouraging the next generation to keep fighting for human rights, equality, and justice.

➤ Analysis of successful gender equality policies implemented globally

Equal rights for women and men should be a top priority for any society that wants to thrive economically and socially. Over the years, several nations have enacted laws and programs to remove structural impediments to women's empowerment and advancement and to advance gender parity. This article examines effective global policies for gender equality, examining their constituent parts, social effects, and lessons for accelerating progress toward global gender parity.

Sweden, Norway, Finland, Denmark, and Iceland are among the Nordic countries lauded for their progressive social policies that support women's rights. Affordable and high-quality child care, paid and unpaid parental leave, work-life balance, and equal educational opportunity are all a part of these policies. These countries make it possible for women to work full-time while still tending to their families because of the extensive network of social services available to them. Gender equality initiatives, as illustrated by the Nordic model, need to take into account both institutional and cultural barriers.

High rates of female labor force participation, narrower wage discrepancies between men and women, and more women in top positions are all outcomes of the Nordic model. High placement on international measures of gender equality attest to the efficacy of these countries' comprehensive response to the issue.

When it comes to policies promoting gender equality, Rwanda stands out as a leading example. At least 30 percent of legislative seats are set aside by law to be designated for women. Rwanda now has one of the world's highest percentages of women in parliament as a result of this forward-thinking policy.

The implementation of gender quotas in politics has resulted in greater female participation, louder female voices, and a greater impact on public policy. Rwanda's example shows that quotas and other affirmative action measures can speed up the process of reaching gender parity in positions of power.

3: Certification of Equal Pay in Iceland
Equal pay certification is an innovative solution to the gender pay gap that has been used in Iceland. Companies and organizations are required to conduct equal pay audits, ensuring that men and women receive equal compensation for equivalent labor. Any company that cannot prove pay equity will be fined.

An important factor in narrowing the wage difference between men and women is Iceland's certification system for equal pay. This policy sets an example for other countries to follow by making businesses responsible for pay discrepancies and increasing workplace transparency and fairness.

4 Canada: Budgeting for Women and Men
Gender budgeting, in which the effects of budgetary decisions on women and men are separately considered and resources

are allocated to close gender gaps, has been adopted in Canada. By prioritizing activities and programs that specifically help women and underrepresented groups, gender budgeting helps to ensure that government expenditure is in line with gender equality goals.

The impact of gender budgeting may be seen in the increased funding for programs that directly help women, such as those for higher education, healthcare, child care, and vocational education and training. This method ensures that government policies are adapted to meet the specific needs of women, which boosts their economic and social standing.

Changes to Customary Law in Namibia
The government of Namibia has made great strides in advancing women's rights through its efforts to change traditional laws that upheld discrimination based on gender. Traditional conventions that suppressed women's rights within families and communities have been challenged by legal developments that have provided women greater power over property, inheritance, and marital decisions.

The effects of the customary law reforms in Namibia have been positive in many ways, especially for women's economic and social status. These changes have helped create a more gender-balanced society by addressing long-standing inequalities.

Several important takeaways from the analysis of these effective measures for gender equality are highlighted:

Policies that are effective in combating gender disparity take a holistic approach by addressing not just one aspect of the problem but several. Comprehensive techniques are crucial for establishing permanent change.

Gender quotas and other forms of affirmative action have been shown to be successful in boosting the number of women in leadership positions. They make possibilities available to women that would be inaccessible owing to structural biases.

Fair treatment and equitable chances in the workplace can be promoted by making pay structures and policies public and holding companies accountable for them. Compliance can be ensured by legal mandates and certification systems.

Budgeting that takes gender into account is called gender responsive budgeting, and it's used to pinpoint inequalities and direct funding toward programs that advance gender parity. Government expenditure should be gender-balanced, and gender budgeting helps make that happen.

Challenges to entrenched gender norms require both cultural sensitivity and legal reforms in order to effectively address discriminatory customary practices. In traditional settings, such changes can give women more agency.

Successful policies must include education and awareness campaigns that promote gender equality education and women's rights. Gender equality activities can flourish in an atmosphere of mutual understanding and shattered assumptions fostered by education.

Conclusion

The world over, proactive steps, legal reforms, and all-encompassing approaches to achieving gender equality have proven their revolutionary impact. In addition to advancing women's rights, these policies have helped create more welcoming, equitable, and prosperous communities for all people. By studying these achievements, governments around the world may develop and enact policies that advance women's rights, boost women's economic participation, and make the world a better place for all people. Societies may create a future in which gender equality is not merely a policy aim but a fundamental reality for all if they persist in their efforts, collaborate, and commit to equality.

➤ Exploration of grassroots movements and their role in promoting social justice

Throughout history, grassroots movements have been crucial in advancing social justice and propelling societal change because they are fueled by the passion and resolve of everyday people. These grassroots groups are targeting a wide range of concerns, from civil liberties and environmental fairness to gender parity and economic autonomy. This article examines the role grassroots movements have in advancing social justice and creating more equitable and welcoming communities.

Roots in History Grassroots movements have a long and storied history, frequently forming in reaction to social wrongs and unequal treatment. In the United States, we have the Civil Rights Movement; in South Africa, we have the anti-apartheid movement; and all across the world, there are labor movements fighting for workers' rights. These movements brought together people of many backgrounds to fight against oppressive regimes, spurred on by a desire for social reform and equality.

Racial justice, environmental protection, LGBTQ+ rights, indigenous rights, and economic equality are just a few of the many topics that grassroots movements support. The interconnectedness of social justice concerns is highlighted by the fact that each movement is rooted in the specific experiences and challenges experienced by the communities it represents.

Second, plans and community mobilization

Participation in the Community: Grassroots movements have strong relationships to the people they want to help. By holding town hall meetings, workshops, and dialogue sessions, they bring the community together and give them a feeling of shared purpose. Community members' voices are heard and respected by grassroots organizers, who use that information to tailor their efforts to the needs of the people they claim to serve.

Advocacy and Awareness: Grassroots movements use grassroots media, social media campaigns, rallies, and nonviolent protests to bring attention to social justice problems. They work to change policies, hold institutions accountable, and combat discrimination through peaceful means. To increase their effectiveness, grassroots organizers frequently work with lawyers, academics, and government officials.

Education and Empowerment Grassroots movements equip community people with knowledge and tools. Individuals are given the knowledge and resources to effectively advocate for their rights through workshops, training sessions, and skill-building programs. Those working at the grassroots level seek to develop local leaders and inspire the next wave of activists and advocates.

3. Results and Influence

Reforms in government policy have resulted from grassroots movements on the local, national, and global levels. Advocacy efforts have led to the implementation of anti-discrimination laws, environmental restrictions, and social welfare measures that address systemic imbalances. By relentlessly advocating for policies that would benefit underprivileged communities, grassroots movements have pushed policymakers to prioritize social justice problems.

Attitude and perception changes are often sparked by grassroots movements' rejection of conventional wisdom. Through education and open discussion, these groups work to eliminate bias and foster a more accepting culture for all people.

Strengthening Community Ties and Social Cohesion Grassroots movements have this effect. These movements foster networks of support and solidarity by rallying people of the community around common aims. Members of a community can discover strength and a place to call home inside grassroots movements, which can help them become more self-reliant and united.

Issues to Address and Future Thoughts
When it comes to money and manpower, grassroots groups sometimes have to make do with what they have. Despite these caveats, they nevertheless have a considerable effect. Volunteer efforts are most likely to succeed and endure if they get financial backing from donors, philanthropic organizations, and governments.

Guaranteeing inclusiveness within grass-roots movements is essential. Acknowledging the interconnectedness of social justice concerns, including race, gender, sexuality, and economic status, is vital. To prevent internal marginalization, movements must aggressively embrace voices and opinions from across the political spectrum.

Long-term effects require sustainable methods, which only grassroots movements can provide. Sustaining the momentum and impact of social justice programs requires building alliances, cooperating with established groups, and cultivating leaders at the grassroots level. Keeping the momentum of grassroots movements for social justice alive can be aided by education and awareness activities.

Conclusion

Social change and justice can be catalyzed effectively by grassroots movements that draw on the energy and enthusiasm of everyday people. They are essential in the fight for a more just and inclusive society because of their ability to galvanize communities, combat structural injustices, and push for policy changes. The importance of grassroots movements in creating a more equitable, empathic, and compassionate world can be understood by recognizing their varied beginnings, tactics, and outcomes.

It is crucial for individuals, communities, and institutions to support and amplify the work of grassroots movements as we consider their successes and the difficulties they encounter. By supporting grassroots activists, speaking up for their causes, and creating a space where their voices are heard and appreciated, society may water the seeds of social justice and grow it into a sustainable movement that benefits everyone.

➤ Case studies of countries or regions making significant progress in gender equality

As a reflection of a society's dedication to equity, justice, and human rights, gender parity is an important barometer of development and advancement. While there are still many obstacles to overcome, many countries and regions have achieved significant progress toward gender equality in many arenas. This article looks at specific examples of countries and areas that have made substantial strides toward gender equality and analyzes the circumstances, laws, and activities that have led to these achievements.

The Nordic Region: An Early Adopter of Women's Rights
For context, the Nordic countries—Sweden, Norway, Finland, Denmark, and Iceland—are held up as leaders in the fight for gender parity. These nations have put in place extensive laws to combat discrimination against women in the workplace, lack of maternity leave, inadequate child care, and underrepresentation of women in government.

Important Steps:
Parental leave rules in the Nordic countries are generous, and they allow both parents to take turns caring for their children. This encourages a fairer division of housework and paves the way for more women to enter the labor sector.
Childcare is easily accessible and reasonably priced, allowing more mothers to participate in the labor field without sacrificing the well-being of their children.

Many Nordic countries have instituted gender quotas in politics and on business boards to ensure that women are adequately represented. These quotas have considerably improved women's political engagement and leadership roles in the corporate sector.

The actions taken by the Nordic countries have had a significant impact, as seen by the narrow salary difference between men and women, the high rate of female labor force participation, and the large number of women holding positions of power in business and government. These countries consistently perform well on international measures of gender equality and can therefore be used as examples elsewhere.

Rwandan Women's Political Empowerment

Rwanda, a small country in East Africa, has made great strides toward achieving gender parity, especially in elected office. After the country's horrific genocide in 1994, the government of Rwanda implemented progressive policies to strengthen the role of women and reconstruct the country.

Important Steps:

The Rwandan government instituted a quota system mandating the reservation of at least 30% of parliamentary seats for women. As a direct result of these efforts, Rwanda now has one of the world's highest representations of female lawmakers.

Leadership programs for women have been organized by the government and non-governmental organizations (NGOs) to increase the number of women in positions of political and administrative power.

The implementation of gender quotas in Rwanda has resulted in a dramatic rise in the number of women holding public office, leading to a more representative government. The progress and post-conflict reconciliation of Rwanda may be traced in large part to the contributions of women who hold major decision-making positions in the country.

Getting to Zero: The Gender Pay Gap in Iceland

The gender pay gap is a chronic problem in many societies, and Iceland has been at the forefront of measures to overcome it. The country's proactive strategy to ensure equal pay for equal work is indicative of its dedication to gender equality.

Important Steps:

Companies in Iceland are required to provide evidence that they provide equal pay for their male and female employees through the Equal Pay Certification system. Any company that cannot prove pay equity will be fined.

Salary information is required to be disclosed by companies, which fosters openness and responsibility in compensation plans.

Effect: Women in Iceland are paid at least as much as males for doing the same work thanks to a certification system and steps to increase transparency. By enforcing responsibility on business owners, Iceland has shown how to deal with wage inequality in a way that other countries can learn from.

4 - Women's Economic Empowerment in Bangladesh

Bangladesh is a country in South Asia that has made great strides in advancing women's rights, especially in the textile and garment industry.

Important Steps:

The textile and garment industry in Bangladesh has given millions of women a chance to work and improve their economic standing. The transformation of traditional gender norms has been greatly aided by initiatives to increase the number of women in the labor force.

Training and Skill Development: Non-governmental organizations and government programs provide training and skill development efforts, giving women the tools they need to succeed in fields like textiles and manufacturing.

As a result, women in Bangladesh are now more financially independent, have higher standards of life, and enjoy greater gender equality than ever before. The advancement and flourishing of the country's economy can be directly attributed to the efforts of its working women.

Conclusion

Case studies of countries and places that have made substantial strides toward gender equality shed light on the wide range of approaches that have led to such gains. These examples highlight the significance of focused initiatives and systemic reforms in advancing gender equality, and they range from comprehensive regulations covering many areas of gender inequality to proactive measures like gender quotas and equal pay certification.

While there has been some success, there is still more work to be done, and no silver bullet exists. Approaches tailored to the individual circumstances of each community are necessary. Promoting gender equality on a worldwide scale requires the combined efforts of governments, civil society organizations, corporations, and international organizations.

Societies may speed up their progress toward gender equality by studying these case studies and adopting innovative, inclusive policies. Creating a more equal world in which every person, regardless of gender, has the opportunity to prosper and contribute meaningfully to society requires economic empowerment for women, increased political representation, and the elimination of discriminatory behaviors. Societies may create a future where gender equality is not only an ideal but a lived reality for all via persistent efforts and concerted action.

Chapter 6: Building a Balanced Future: Challenges and Opportunities

➤ Current challenges in achieving gender equality and social justice

Gender parity and social justice continue to be major issues for communities around the globe. The achievement of these aims remains elusive despite substantial advances in recent decades. This essay investigates the systemic problems, cultural obstacles, and long-standing disparities that prevent progress toward gender equality and social justice.

1. Prejudice based on gender
Discrimination against women and gender minorities persists in many ways, including but not limited to pay gap, educational opportunity, and underrepresentation in positions of power. Progress toward equality is hampered by pervasive gender bias, which serves to legitimize discriminatory social norms.

Persistent and harmful gender norms contribute significantly to existing inequities. Gender stereotypes limit women's participation in politics, the workplace, and formal education. In order to create a more just and inclusive society, it is crucial that these preconceptions be challenged.

2 Gender-Based Violence and Violence Against Women
Domestic violence, sexual harassment, and human trafficking are all forms of gender-based violence that continue to be

serious problems today. Gender-based violence not only violates human rights but also promotes power disparities, maintaining a cycle of fear and silence among victims.

Victims of gender-based violence are sometimes not adequately protected by the law because of weak legal systems and weak enforcement mechanisms. Improving legal safeguards, expanding access to help, and increasing public understanding are all crucial in the fight against this ubiquitous problem.

3 Discrimination in the Workplace and Income Inequality
Women still earn less than men do for equivalent work, despite efforts to close the gender pay gap. Gender pay gap persists due to discrimination in employment, promotion, and compensation.
Women, especially those living in underdeveloped nations, confront stumbling blocks while trying to gain access to economic possibilities like loans, property, and mentoring programs. Financial inclusion can be achieved and these obstacles removed through economic empowerment efforts.

4 Inequities in Health Care and the Right to Have Children
Disparities in Healthcare: Throughout the world, there exist persistent gaps in healthcare access and quality between men and women. Obstacles prevent many women from receiving lifesaving medical care, especially in the areas of maternity and reproductive health.
Women's reproductive rights, especially the right to an abortion in a safe environment, continue to be a divisive topic

in many countries. Women's reproductive rights are inadequately protected, limiting their agency over their own bodies and reproductive decisions.

Multiplying the effects of prejudice and exclusion, intersectionality refers to the ways in which social categories such as race, gender, class, and sexual orientation interact with one another. Because women from marginalized groups experience many forms of discrimination, it might be difficult to meet their specific needs.

Culture and religion: Cultural and religious traditions often reinforce existing power structures and limit women's rights by intersecting with gender discrimination. It takes subtle ways to social change to challenge these conventions without alienating any group.

6. Cyberbullying and online harassment

Online harassment and cyberbullying disproportionately affect women and members of other marginalized groups; this phenomenon is known as digital gender-based violence. While social media has enabled greater worldwide communication, it has also become a breeding ground for sex-based violence, which poses serious threats to users' physical and emotional well-being when interacting online.

Combating impunity: Finding solutions to online harassment calls for coordinated efforts from the tech industry, government, and civil society. In order to ensure accountability and safeguard victims, it is crucial to take action against impunity for cyber-based gender-based violence.

Conclusion

Collective effort, legal reforms, cultural adjustments, and educational activities are all necessary to advance gender equality and social justice. The difficulties highlighted in this essay highlight the critical need to overcome long-standing biases, discriminatory practices, and systemic imbalances. To remove obstacles, test preconceived notions, and spread acceptance, it will take the combined efforts of governments, civil society organizations, enterprises, and individuals.

To combat prejudice and promote tolerance and compassion, educational and awareness efforts are necessary. Dismantling discriminatory practices requires legal reforms that protect the rights of women and gender minorities, as well as rigorous enforcement procedures. A more fair society, where people can prosper without fear of prejudice or violence, can only be achieved by increasing women's economic, political, and social empowerment.

When societies recognize and address these issues head-on, they pave the way for a future in which gender equality and social justice are not just ideals, but actual experiences for people of all genders, backgrounds, and identities. A more just and equal society, where everyone's rights and dignity are respected, can be fostered over time by tireless activism, education, and empathy.

➢ Analysis of the role of education and awareness in fostering change

The importance of education and awareness to bring about societal change, combat prejudice, and foster acceptance cannot be overstated. Awareness campaigns create empathy, understanding, and collective action, while education prepares individuals with knowledge and the ability to think critically. This essay examines the impact of education and knowledge on gender equality, environmental protection, social justice, and cultural tolerance, among other topics, as a means of creating change.

1. The Influence of Education on Individual Minds
Encouragement of Learning: Schooling is Crucial to Social Advancement. Societies enable individuals, especially those from marginalized groups, to escape poverty, get access to opportunities, and make important contributions to society at large when education is both widely available and of high quality.

Critical Thinking and Empathy: Education cultivates critical thinking abilities, enabling individuals to question social conventions, challenge preconceptions, and evaluate difficult issues. Learning to accept other people's cultures, beliefs, and worldviews is made easier when they are exposed to these perspectives.

Education is a critical factor in advancing gender parity. Gender stereotypes can be broken down and girls and women's confidence can be bolstered via education. Curricula can also be created to encourage diversity and gender equality from a young age by critiquing stereotypical gender roles.

The Influence of Public Opinion on Awareness Generation
Educating the Public: Environmental protection, mental health, LGBTQ+ rights, and racial equality are just a few of the causes that have benefited greatly from awareness campaigns. These initiatives spark debate, confront prejudice, and provoke introspection, all of which contribute to a more progressive culture.

Environmental Conservation: Environmental awareness campaigns educate the public about climate change, biodiversity loss, and sustainable practices. Humans can have a positive effect on the environment if more people are aware of the link between their actions and the state of the planet.

Campaigns to raise public consciousness about social justice concerns including racial discrimination, police brutality, and economic inequality help to expose these pervasive problems. These campaigns challenge established norms, rally public support, and hold institutions accountable, pushing advocacy for policy reforms and societal change.

Third, Cultural Acceptance Education and Awareness
Education's promotion of cultural awareness and acceptance is central to its mission. Learning about and respecting one another's cultural background is crucial in today's more multicultural communities. By highlighting the many different

cultures represented in their student bodies, schools may help foster an environment of acceptance and tolerance.

Public opinion can be changed by awareness programs that target preconceptions and stereotypes in a certain culture. These commercials build a more tolerant and inclusive society by recognizing commonalities while also showing the variety of different cultures.

Technology and social media's impact on society
Education in the digital age: because to technological advancements, knowledge may now be gained by anybody, wherever in the globe. Learning never stops, and neither do online courses, educational platforms, or electronic publications. Programs that use digital tools to educate people help those who would otherwise not have access to education.

The use of social media for awareness purposes is particularly effective since it allows campaigns to reach a much wider audience. Awareness-raising online movements are often sparked by hashtags, viral videos, and social media challenges. Grass-roots activism is facilitated by social media because individuals may more easily organize support and lobby for reform.

Difficulties and Things to Think About
Disinformation and misinformation are problems that have emerged with the advent of the digital age. Confusion and the reinforcement of prejudice can be the result of false narratives, which can hinder educational efforts and awareness

campaigns. Addressing disinformation involves media literacy education and critical thinking abilities to separate trustworthy sources from misinformation.

Quality education and awareness initiatives continue to face barriers to access, especially in underserved or out-of-the-way areas. Educational resources and awareness campaigns may have limited impact due to socioeconomic hurdles, inadequate infrastructure, and digital divides. In order to encourage widespread change, it is crucial to work toward ensuring equitable access.

Respect for cultural norms and practices: Different cultural settings call for different approaches to learning and advocacy. All methods must be developed with sensitivity to and appreciation for local culture. Education and awareness initiatives that are designed to appeal to a wide range of cultures are more likely to succeed in their goals of increasing people's openness to new ideas.

Conclusion

Awareness and understanding are crucial resources for advancing social justice, combating prejudice, and creating a more accepting and equitable society. Education gives people the tools they need to question and change the status quo in their communities. On the other hand, awareness campaigns can help people feel compassion, motivate groups to take action, and combat long-held prejudices.

Technology and social media in the modern day have greatly expanded the reach of instructional materials and awareness campaigns, breaking down geographical barriers and giving rise to international movements for positive change. However, obstacles like inaccuracy, accessibility, and cultural sensitivity need to be overcome to guarantee the success of such endeavors.

Societies may cultivate a future that is more enlightened, tolerant, and inclusive by spending money on education, creating awareness campaigns, and using technology in a responsible manner. Building a world where everyone is valued, respected, and given the opportunity to thrive requires a foundation of social transformation, which may be achieved by equipping individuals with knowledge, empathy, and understanding. A more just, egalitarian, and compassionate world can be fostered for all via civilizations' persistent efforts in education and awareness.

➢ Exploration of the potential of technology in advancing gender equality

The rise of digital technologies has made them a potent tool for advancing social justice and gender parity. The revolutionary power of technology lies in its ability to bridge gaps, magnify voices, and disrupt old norms. In this essay, we'll look at the many ways in which technological advancements can help bring about gender equality, from expanding opportunities for girls and women to get an education and healthcare to fostering gender-sensitive policymaking and reducing the prevalence of violence against women.

Lifelong learning and educational equity
Through the use of online platforms, people all over the world now have access to education. By providing access to a wide variety of courses, online learning environments are boosting the educational and professional opportunities available to women, particularly in underprivileged areas. Women can study and care for their families and careers because to the adaptability of these platforms.

Initiatives to promote digital literacy provide women with the fundamental computer and internet skills necessary to compete in today's global economy. Women's self-esteem is boosted when they are able to successfully use the internet for research, enhance their education, and advocate for causes they care about.

2. Economic Independence and Business Creation

Technology has opened up new opportunities for women business owners in the realm of e-commerce and online marketplaces. Women who own their own businesses or who are self-employed in the arts or crafts can reach a global audience by showcasing their wares online. E-commerce helps people become economically self-sufficient since it opens up new avenues of commerce and employment.

Mobile banking, digital wallets, and online payment systems have paved the way for women to participate in the financial mainstream, especially in areas with limited access to traditional banking services. Women are less reliant on men to handle money, gain access to credit, and take part in economic activities thanks to digital payments.

Advancing Women's Economic Independence
Flexibility in scheduling and the ability to work from home have become more commonplace in today's business as a result of technological advancements. These modifications help women by permitting them to hold down both paid and unpaid caring roles. By allowing women, especially mothers and caregivers, to work remotely, we can help advance gender parity in the workplace.

Artificial intelligence (AI) methods can be used to study and correct for gender bias in areas such as hiring and employee reviews. AI algorithms can help eliminate biased language in job descriptions and assess candidates based on skills and credentials, supporting fair hiring practices and diversity in the workforce.

4. Reproductive and Health Care Rights

Access to medical treatment, especially in outlying locations, has been enhanced by the rise of telemedicine and mobile health apps. These technologies allow women to consult healthcare specialists, obtain medical advice, and check their health remotely. Improved mental health treatments, expanded reproductive health options, and better maternal care are all possible because to telemedicine.

Information on reproductive health, family planning, and sexual education is available via mobile apps and internet platforms. Women are better able to exercise their reproductive rights, gain access to contraception, and organize their families with the help of these tools. The internet removes barriers to women's access to contraception and other reproductive health services.

Fifth, advocate for gender-sensitive legislation and policy

With the help of data analytics and machine learning, large datasets may be analyzed to reveal gender inequalities in a variety of fields, which can then be used to inform policy decisions. Policymakers can close the gender gap with the help of data-driven insights that reveal the extent of the problem. Targeted interventions are easier to construct with the use of technology, and this guarantees that women's specific issues are addressed in policy.

internet Advocacy and Awareness: Social media and internet platforms serve as important tools for feminist activism and advocacy. Gender-based violence, discrimination, and breaches of reproductive rights are brought to light by MeToo and other online petitions. To effect societal and legislative change, social media campaigns elevate women's voices, rally public support, and hold institutions responsible.

6. Ending Violence Against Women

Women may get rapid help in dangerous situations thanks to safety applications that have panic buttons, GPS monitoring, and emergency hotlines. These apps allow women to speak with authorities or trusted contacts in a covert manner, making them feel more comfortable and secure. For women who are victims of domestic violence or sexual harassment, technology can be a lifeline.

Survivors of gender-based violence have access to online resources such as chat rooms and message boards where they can find comfort and guidance. Because of the confidentiality of these programs, victims can seek assistance without worrying about retaliation. By providing a safe space for survivors to connect with one another and discover information and emotional support, online support groups can help individuals heal and regain their strength.

Difficulties and Things to Think About

The term "digital gender divide" is used to describe the gap that exists between men and women when it comes to their use of and proficiency with digital technologies. Women's access to technology, particularly mobile devices, computers, and the internet, is severely hampered in many parts of the world. Interventions, infrastructure, and digital literacy initiatives are all needed to narrow the digital gender gap.

Problems like cyberbullying and online harassment have emerged alongside the expansion of digital communication channels, with a disproportionate impact on women and members of underrepresented sex groups. Strong cybersecurity measures, regulatory frameworks to address digital gender-based violence, and social media platform accountability in combatting online harassment are all necessary for ensuring online safety.

When it comes to reproductive health services, healthcare apps, and online support platforms, it is especially important to protect women's privacy and data protection. Safeguarding women's personal information and encouraging their continued use of technology-enabled services depends critically on safe data storage, encryption, and informed consent methods.

Women's access to technology and online places may be hampered by entrenched cultural norms and patriarchal attitudes. Women's participation in the digital sphere can't progress until it's widely accepted in society. Traditional obstacles can be countered and inclusiveness can be promoted through awareness campaigns opposing preconceptions and pushing for women's digital rights.

Conclusion

Technology has enormous potential to promote gender equality by providing novel approaches to addressing persistent problems that have historically disadvantaged women around the world. A catalyst for social change, technology has improved access to education, economic opportunity, and gender-sensitive policymaking. However, effectively utilizing technology requires attention to cultural norms, online safety, and the digital gender gap.

Women's empowerment, the elimination of gender disparities, and a more just and equitable world are all possible thanks to the revolutionary potential of technology. To fully realize technology's potential in furthering gender equality, efforts must be made to close technological gaps, increase digital literacy, and promote women's rights in the digital arena. Through collaborative initiatives, innovative solutions, and a dedication to inclusivity, technology can play a crucial role in establishing a future where every woman has the opportunity to thrive, engage fully in society, and contribute meaningfully to the digital age.

➤ Strategies and recommendations for individuals, communities, and governments to promote a balanced world

Achieving a balanced world, where equality, justice, and opportunity are accessible to all regardless of gender, ethnicity, or financial background, needs joint efforts from individuals, communities, and governments. This essay delves into methods and suggestions for creating a more equitable world, touching on topics including women's rights, racial harmony, ecological responsibility, and economic autonomy. A more peaceful and just world is possible if we all do our part, both as individuals and as members of communities and as citizens of governments.

1 Advancing Women's Equality and Economic Independence
Educational initiatives that support girls' education and encourage them to pursue careers in STEM (science, technology, engineering, and mathematics) can help eliminate gender bias and put women at the forefront of sectors that have historically been dominated by males. Girls and young women can have an easier time getting an education if scholarships, mentorship programs, and awareness campaigns are made available to them.

Policies that promote gender equality in the workplace can be implemented by businesses and organizations. These policies can include things like equal pay for equal work, open and honest promotion procedures, and family-friendly provisions such as flexible work hours and parental leave. Eliminating discrimination based on gender in hiring and promotion is crucial to building diverse and welcoming workplaces.

Participation from the Community: Workshops, seminars, and awareness campaigns can be organized to help combat gender stereotypes and spread the message of gender equality. Women can benefit from the safe space provided by community-based groups that offer support services for victims of gender-based violence.

Legislation, regulations, and initiatives backed by the government play a pivotal role in advancing gender parity. Equal pay, access to quality, low-cost childcare, and the enforcement of anti-discrimination legislation are all crucial. Women can achieve economic independence with the help of government subsidies, loans, and training programs for entrepreneurs.

2 Promoting Equality and Social Justice

Educational Reform: Education is a great tool for advancing social fairness. Learning about other people's experiences and history might help kids develop empathy and tolerance. Equal access to education can also be achieved through the provision of financial aid and scholarships by academic institutions for students from low-income backgrounds.

Rehabilitative rather than punitive approaches should be prioritized in any proposed criminal justice reform. A more fair and compassionate criminal justice system can be achieved through alternative sentencing programs, inmate mental health support, and recidivism reduction measures.

Those in need, such as the homeless, refugees, and the LGBTQ+ community, might benefit from community-based support systems. The aid and resources offered by community centers, shelters, and counseling services are invaluable. Awareness and action on social justice issues can also be sparked by grassroots efforts like volunteering and advocacy.

Policy Changes: Governments should place a high priority on policies that work to reduce socioeconomic inequalities, such as those that expand access to affordable housing, healthcare, and other types of social assistance. Promoting diversity requires policies that safeguard the rights of underrepresented groups like immigrants, people of color, and the LGBTQ+ community.

3. environmentally-friendly procedures

Sustainable behaviors can be encouraged through environmental education, which aims to increase public understanding of environmental problems and the value of conservation. Programs teaching people about climate change, biodiversity, and sustainable living should be funded by schools, nonprofits, and governments.

Promoting Renewable Energy: Governments can stimulate the adoption of renewable energy sources such as solar, wind, and hydroelectric power. Businesses and individuals can be incentivized to make the switch to sustainable energy by providing subsidies, tax credits, and grants for research.

Communities and people alike can play a role in advancing efforts to reduce garbage and increase recycling rates. Pollution in the environment can be mitigated and natural resources preserved through initiatives like recycling programs, community cleanups, and the promotion of eco-friendly lifestyle choices. Sustainable waste management can be further encouraged by government rules and incentives for recycling enterprises.

Protected areas, wildlife reserves, and marine sanctuaries are some of the tools governments can use to preserve natural resources and biodiversity. Responsible tourism and community-led conservation efforts can help protect ecosystems and wildlife in peril. Conservation and responsible resource management are topics that can be addressed by public awareness campaigns.

4Financial Independence and Poverty Reduction
Governments and communities may encourage entrepreneurship by helping those with promising business ideas get the skills, mentorship, and funding they need to get their ventures off the ground, especially if they come from disadvantaged backgrounds. Microfinance initiatives and business incubators should be easily accessible to the general public.

Job Training and Skill Development: Job training programs that focus on in-demand skills can boost employability among vulnerable populations. By working together, governments, schools, and companies can ensure that people are receiving the most relevant education and training possible to meet the demands of the labor market.

Governments should provide generous social safety nets such as unemployment insurance, medical insurance, and housing subsidies for people and families who are experiencing financial difficulties. These safeguards serve as a cushion for when times are tough, ensuring that people can continue to meet their most fundamental needs.

Promoting ethical business practices and buying fair trade goods is an effective way to help disadvantaged people in developing countries. With fair trade, manufacturers are guaranteed decent pay and secure working conditions. Fair trade goods can be supported by communities and people alike through purchasing decisions and education efforts.

Conclusion

Advancing global harmony calls for a comprehensive strategy that takes into account issues of gender equality, social justice, environmental preservation, and economic imbalances. Everyone from individuals to groups to governments can and should contribute to this effort in their own distinctive ways. Societies may build a more balanced and equitable society for present and future generations by creating economic possibilities, campaigning for social justice, supporting sustainable environmental practices, and educating their members about these issues.

It is crucial for people to take initiative in their communities by volunteering and lending their support to programs that advance diversity and inclusion. In turn, communities can provide safe spaces that help marginalized people and promote mutual respect and tolerance. Governments, as guardians of the public good, have an obligation to enact policies that advance equality, sustainability, and economic opportunity for all citizens.

The future may be shaped by individuals, communities, and governments working together to ensure that everyone has equal access to harmony, fairness, and opportunity. Societies may create a future based on equality, fairness, and shared wealth via persistent efforts, advocacy, and teamwork.

Conclusion:

Societies undergo radical change in the direction of greater equality, inclusion, and harmony as they work toward a society in which gender parity and social justice reign. This in-depth debate sheds light on the difficulties that people, communities, and governments encounter in the pursuit of gender equality and social justice by examining these concerns and proposing solutions and recommendations for creating change. It also brings to light the group work that is needed to overcome these obstacles and make the world a place where everyone may succeed, regardless of their gender, ethnicity, heritage, or identity.

Social justice and gender parity are inextricably linked. Gender discrimination is a social injustice that feeds into and exacerbates other forms of inequality. Systemic inequalities are exacerbated by discrimination based on gender, ethnicity, class, and other characteristics. To create holistic solutions that get at the causes of inequality, it is crucial to first acknowledge the overlaps that exist.

Importance of Knowledge and Understanding:
Change can be accelerated by learning and awareness. The ability to think critically and question biases is a key benefit of education, as is the development of interpersonal skills. Mobilizing communities to support marginalized groups and advance social justice projects, awareness campaigns cultivate empathy, understanding, and collective action.

The Potential of Technology to Transform Lives

When technology is used to further the causes of social justice and gender parity, new doors of opportunity open. Technology has enabled people to educate themselves at their own pace, have their voices heard by a wider audience, and organize on a global scale through online education, digital literacy programs, and social media activism and support networks. However, tackling the digital gender divide, maintaining online safety, and protecting privacy are critical issues in leveraging technology's potential for positive change.

Aiding People, Neighborhoods, and Governments
Individuals are empowered when they are instilled with a sense of pride, competence, and control. The role of communities in providing safety nets, encouraging acceptance, and combating discrimination is crucial. As guardians of the common good, governments are tasked with enacting and implementing regulations that safeguard citizens' rights, eliminate structural discrimination, and expand economic opportunity.

Seeking a More Equilibrium in the World:
In a fair and equitable society, people of all sexes and socioeconomic backgrounds have the same possibilities in life. Empathy and compassion win out over bigotry and intolerance, and all perspectives are valued and respected. To strike this equilibrium, society as a whole must work to eliminate discriminatory practices, question accepted norms, and provide conditions in which all members can flourish.

While many positive strides have been made toward achieving gender parity and social justice, there is still much work to be done. Institutionalized discrimination, cultural norms, and individual biases all act as roadblocks to growth. Consistent efforts at education, activism, policy reform, and community involvement are needed to meet these difficulties. It necessitates a dedication to eliminating oppressive systems, giving a voice to the voiceless, and promoting tolerance and compassion.

In sum, a rallying cry for change:
Finally, progress toward gender parity and social justice is not merely an aspirational ideal. To create a world in which every person may live a life of dignity, free from prejudice and injustice, calls for unyielding dedication, cooperative action, and a shared commitment. It calls for bravery in the face of wrongdoing, compassion for others, and resolve to effect change that will last.

Let us proceed with the conviction that a future in which all people can thrive can be more than a pipe dream. We can pave the way for a future where gender equality and social justice are not just ideals but actual experiences by welcoming difference, fostering inclusion, and fighting for the rights of every person. Let us continue this important task together so that future generations can inherit a society where equality and social justice are the norm.

www.ingramcontent.com/pod-product-compliance
Lightning Source LLC
LaVergne TN
LVHW020444070526
838199LV00063B/4844